A VOICE FROM
OLD NEW YORK

Books by Louis Auchincloss

◇◇◇ FICTION ◇◇◇

THE INDIFFERENT CHILDREN

THE INJUSTICE COLLECTORS

SYBIL

A LAW FOR THE LION

THE ROMANTIC EGOISTS

THE GREAT WORLD AND TIMOTHY COLT

VENUS IN SPARTA

PURSUIT OF THE PRODIGAL

THE HOUSE OF FIVE TALENTS

PORTRAIT IN BROWNSTONE

POWERS OF ATTORNEY

THE RECTOR OF JUSTIN

THE EMBEZZLER

TALES OF MANHATTAN

A WORLD OF PROFIT

SECOND CHANCE

I COME AS A THIEF

THE PARTNERS

THE WINTHROP COVENANT

THE DARK LADY

THE COUNTRY COUSIN

THE HOUSE OF THE PROPHET

THE CAT AND THE KING

A VOICE FROM OLD NEW YORK

A Memoir of My Youth

Louis Auchincloss

HOUGHTON MIFFLIN HARCOURT

Boston ||| *New York* ||| 2010

Copyright © 2010 by Louis Auchincloss

For information about permission to reproduce
selections from this book, write to Permissions,
Houghton Mifflin Harcourt Publishing Company,
215 Park Avenue South, New York, New York 10003.

WWW.HMHBOOKS.COM

Library of Congress Cataloging-in-Publication Data
Auchincloss, Louis.
A voice from old New York : a memoir of
my youth / Louis Auchincloss.
p. cm.
ISBN 978-0-547-34153-8
1. Auchincloss, Louis. 2. Auchincloss,
Louis—Childhood and youth. 3. Authors,
American—20th century—Biography. I. Title.
PS3501.U25Z46   2010
813'.54—dc22   [B]   2010015894

Book design by Patrick Barry

Printed in the United States of America

DOC 10 9 8 7 6 5 4 3 2 1

◇◇◇ CONTENTS ◇◇◇

TURNING BACK

An Introduction

◇◇◇

I walk through the long schoolroom questioning;
A kind old nun in a white hood replies;
The children learn to cipher and to sing,
To study reading-books and histories,
To cut and sew, be neat in everything
In the best modern way — the children's eyes
In momentary wonder stare upon
A sixty-year-old smiling public man.

—William Butler Yeats,
Among School Children

Reading, writing, and talking about books have occupied much of my life, and so, not surprisingly, it is here where I find I must begin.

When I retired from the practice of law at age sixty-nine I had more than enough time for the writing of my novels, and I gladly accepted the offer of my friend James Tuttleton, head of the English department at New York University, to teach there. They had adopted a policy of inviting known authors, without academic qualifications, to give courses, and Tuttleton had in mind that I might give one on Henry James and Edith Wharton, as I had written books on both. Ultimately I did give such a course to a small group of graduate students, but what I had in mind was a more extensive course for undergraduates on Shakespeare and his contemporary dramatists.

I had long wanted to do something to rebut the idiotic theories that the man from Stratford couldn't have written the thirty-seven plays attributed to him. My ambitions were further aroused by a conversation with the brilliant U.S. Supreme Court justice Antonin Scalia who told me that he favored the Earl of Oxford as the true author of Shakespeare's works. Hearing this from such an informed and learned man shocked me considerably. So I drew up a detailed plan for what we might cover that would illustrate my case. Each week, I envisioned, the students would read a play of Shakespeare's, along with something by a contemporary, say, Jonson, Marlowe, Webster, Beaumont and Fletcher, Tourneur, Middleton, or what have you.

My idea was to show that Shakespeare, with his education and background, fitted perfectly into his times; that he wrote for the theatre in much the same way as the others, using similar plots, ideas, and devices. But, in short, I wanted to demonstrate that he was simply so much better than the others that, in his hands, all the conventions seemed new, fresh, and alive. To think his plays were written by Bacon or Oxford is, in my opinion, to show a tin ear.

A man with a tin ear for music has no trouble confessing it, but one with a tin ear for poetry may be genuinely unaware of it. Especially in these, prosaic-at-best, times. Such a reader is aware of hearing the same words that a poetry lover does, and he believes that he gives them the same meaning. What is it then, he must ask himself, that sets the interpretations of experts apart from his own? When Hamlet ends his tragedy with the line "You that look pale and tremble at this chance," the less initiated reader hears only a simple sentence. Why is it experienced readers and scholars hear more and deeper meanings than the newcomer? How does one come to appreciate all these nuances?

When I, attempting to make the seriousness of a judge appear trivial, approached the dean with my project, he looked doubtful. "I know, I know," I said, responding to that look people get when their manners conflict with their purpose. "Shakespeare is sacred territory, and I don't belong to the union."

"Well, what are your qualifications then?"

"I'm a doctor of letters of NYU."

There was a moment of surprised silence before the dean recovered himself. "But that was honorary."

"You should be more careful in handing those things out."

However minimal the dean considered my chances of success, I had won a victory, of sorts. The following fall, I found myself facing some thirty young men and women, only five or six of whom had ever read a play by the bard. That many of them had no ear for poetic language became only too clear when I read their papers, into which it was distressingly common for them to insert, with the stunning confidence of Dickens's er-

rant urchins, plagiarized passages. The fact that they didn't realize that it was impossible for me not to recognize the shift
from their own clumsy prose to that of a more elevated variety
spoke worlds of their difficulties with language. And perhaps
with life.

Would a student deaf to poetry respond to prose? Fortunately Shakespeare wrote both, and I had some success in
reading aloud Hamlet's peerless speech to Rosencrantz and
Guildenstern.

"I have of late, but wherefore I know not, lost all my mirth,
forgone all custom of exercise, and indeed it goes so heavily
with my disposition that this goodly frame, the earth, seems
to me a sterile promontory, this most excellent canopy the air,
look you, this brave overhanging firmament, this majestical
roof fretted with golden fire, why it appears no other thing to
me than a foul and pestilent congregation of vapours."

The unrestrained emotion and humanity of the piece always
stopped the class, at least for a few moments. The students' attention to something so archaically expressed pleased me. It is
something I cheerfully recall when the earth to me, too, seems
a "sterile promontory." I remember how Shakespeare reached
across time to touch their feelings. I cannot claim to expect
any comparable impact. But I believe in words, for their power
to articulate what others have previously sought to communi-
cate, along with their capacity to show us that most terrifying
vantage, ourselves.

I find myself some years past my ninetieth birthday as I approach this task of remembering (or, at other times, continu-

ing, happily, to forget) my life. I cannot say if, like Shakespeare, I am a man who fit perfectly into his times, or if I stood par. Nor can I be sure whether I have, either on the page or in my daily existence, revealed a tin ear for life or art. But I believe I can take you back to those who dominated the places of my youth, and those who shared them. I believe I may try to examine those who, for whatever reasons, never gained admittance to the places I dwelled merely by advantage of birth. This book is not for me, not just, as memoirs sometimes are, a record of my terrors or complaints. It is for those who I have passed my time with, those who showed me that there was much to admire, along with all the others who have made my life, the people I have been fortunate enough to encounter, the voices I remember and would like to introduce to you.

Part I

How It Was

◇◇◇

1

Genealogy, et cetera

O F MANY PEOPLE it does not tell us much to describe them as residents of New York City because so large a portion of those so situated were born and raised elsewhere or are even recent arrivals. In my own case, the description is only too telling, as all eight of my grandparents lived the bulk of their lives in this marvelous place.

I was born in 1917 to parents who had been wed in their early twenties in 1911. My father, Joseph Howland Auchincloss, named for a great uncle who had been a Civil War general, was a member of a prominent New York law firm known by the abbreviated title of Davis Polk. (The senior partner was the former Democratic presidential candidate John W. Davis.) My mother, the former Priscilla Stanton, was a member of a large, close-knit, and socially active clan, the Dixons, who lived in neighboring brownstones on West Forty-ninth Street and summered in shingle villas by the sea in Southampton.

Both of my parents lived to be old and were devoted to their four children, John, Priscilla, myself, and Howland. But a seldom-discussed shadow complicated our lives. My father suffered all his life from severe periodic depressions that sometimes caused him to suspend the practice of law for as much as a year. It was as though something in his spirit simply fell away upon occasion and, whatever his exertions, could not be regained. Yet my father remained charming and popular with the world at large, whatever the cost to himself. We were not raised to show our problems or disappointments in public.

The term "getting ahead" invokes a sacred American goal. Yet it was not one ever much emphasized by my father, who was utterly content with his partners, his practice, his family, and his sports. He had no hankering for political office or other distinction. Until the onslaught of his nervous ailments in late middle age, he seemed as happy as a man could be. And why should he not have been? To support his devoted wife and children he could count, in the year 1931 for example, on the following assets: a modest but ample brownstone in Manhattan; a house in Long Island for weekends and summer; a rented villa in Bar Harbor, Maine, for July; four housemaids; two children's nurses; a couple to maintain the Long Island abode; a chauffeur and four cars; several social clubs; and private schools for the children.

Mother used to warn us when we went to the country for the weekend: "Now don't expect anything fancy; we've just got the couple!" Father would add that "the couple" referred to most often in such circumstances was actually never more than one and a half people. (One always drank and the other was, unfailingly, a treasure.) But even so!

My father managed all of the above on an income of a hundred thousand dollars a year, out of which he managed to make an annual saving. Of course the dollar went further then, but still. Yet it never occurred to me that we were rich. We lived only as other successful lawyers' and doctors' families did.

I was quite aware of who the rich were. They inhabited Beaux Arts mansions rather than brownstones and had butlers and sometimes organs in the front hall. One of Father's uncles had married a Standard Oil heiress. Now *she* was rich. She had thirty in help.

The younger members of my world took the fact that it was supported by armies of domestic servants, like our beloved Maggie, largely for granted. That these domestics were mostly recruited from an Ireland that could no longer support its own we accepted. Without thinking too much about the circumstances. Just as we accepted the brownstone stoops that ascended to our front doors and the lights on stilts that controlled the traffic on Fifth Avenue. I don't recall even discussing with another child the plight of the poor women who lived in narrow cubicles on the often cold top floors of our brownstones and who worked around the clock with one day off a week and nothing to do on it. At Christmas, one heard the parental whispered warning about not giving too much to the maids because "they give it all to the church."

The help weren't the only group often ignored. I didn't meet any Jews until I was sent to Bovee on Fifth Avenue at Sixty-fourth Street, which, unlike the other fashionable boys' day schools of the time, had no restrictions. I don't know why Father selected it, but it had a high reputation and most of the boys came from Protestant families. My time there was a great blessing, for getting to know some Jewish boys made me question the casual anti-Semitism that sprinkled the conversation at home and in the houses of family friends and relations.

I don't recall people (grownups, of course) giving any particular reason for objecting to Jews, except that they were supposed to be grasping in money matters. It simply seemed to be accepted that they were to be avoided at all costs in terms of social mixing. It was as if they carried some easily contractible and unattractive, though not necessarily dangerous, ailment.

Although I neither understood nor sympathized with the prejudice—I liked my Bovee Jewish friends and admired their wealth—I saw that the attitude, however displeasing, was a natural phenomenon of the parents' generation. When we moved our summer residence from Long Island's south to north shore, I gave my friends Father's reason as placidly as if it were a change of weather: "Because of the Jews."

Mother was too intelligent for prejudice but too indifferent to fight it. A friend of my father's attending a reception at the Stantons as a young man told me that he once found my mother, Priscilla, then eighteen, pouting in a corner at some sort of gathering. She complained: "Mother asks all her pet Jews, but won't have mine."

Mother's prejudices were non-denominational. What she complained about in me was my admiration of wealth. "My grandmother's snobbishness has come back to earth in Louis," she used to say.

Her grandmother, born Babcock, had been a rigid, be-wigged old dowager with the rough candor about money of an earlier New York society. "Don't say you don't like Mrs. Kingsland," she once reproached my mother. "She has three million dollars."

The elderly lady was not much impressed by Mother's engagement to an Auchincloss. "I suppose it's better than being the last leaf on the tree" was her comment. She thought of Mother at twenty-one as an old maid! She herself had been married at sixteen.

Despite the fact that there were few with whom she could discuss his depression, Mother gave my father unfailing and needed support. She had no ambition for the glories of the world, but she possessed a strong desire to hang on to the benefits of her family's share of the status quo for her children. She had great faith in the economic opportunities available to her sons if they followed the normal course of their class and fortune. She dreaded their striking out into untested areas.

In all of this she was an average mother; the trouble was that she was not an average woman. She was brilliantly imaginative, well read, and independently daring; *she* should have been the writer in the family. As it was she gave too much of her fine mind to the care of her offspring at the expense of their independence.

But where these children were concerned she was abjectly timid; she deemed it her sacred duty to spare them all risks, emotional and physical. Her fine mind was singularly free of prejudice, but she saw danger to her dependents in the unconventional. And she saw it in any overemphasis on the arts, which she could not justify except in the case of near genius, which she certainly did not recognize in my literary aspirations, with the result that she used all her formidable talents to discourage my writing. She quite sincerely believed she was sparing me the bitterness of failure. But there was in her also a curious pessimism about the ability of her children to achieve success in any field. If one of us fell in love, for example, she tended to assume it would be unrequited.

2

John and Priscilla

MY BROTHER JOHN, six years my senior, was a sober, serious man with a fine clear mind who interrupted a promising career in the State Department to share a life of pleasure and leisure with a rich and devoted wife. Armed with discrimination, taste, and moderation, they achieved both happiness and success in the sort of existence that often offers less than that.

John was a brilliant student at school and college, but he was totally devoid of personal ambition and made not the slightest change in his natural good manners in greeting no matter how famous a visitor. When our cousin Janet Auchincloss (Mrs. Hugh D.), whose daughter Jackie would become first lady, beckoned to him at a crowded Washington party to come and talk to her, he simply shook his head. Asked later to explain this, he told her:

"But Janet, to get near you I have to elbow my rough way through a gaping crowd. I don't do that."

"Look whom you leave me with."

Janet was right. The great are left with the wrong people.

* * *

Once, when I pointed out to my older brother that I found his group in Newport on the stuffy side, he replied that their dinners were good and their guests on time and never inebriated. I retorted that he would have been happy with the formality and regularity of the court of Versailles, and he did not deny it. For a long time it seemed to me that this propriety was inconsistent with a serious life, that such an attitude must indicate a certain triviality of spirit or even of heart. I was wrong.

My brother, you see, needed only himself for an intellectual companion. He was a deep reader and thinker, and a conscientious liberal in a rigidly conservative society to whose tenets he paid no attention but never took the trouble to contradict. When he had to face a long and agonizing death struggle, no one was ever a better or more cheerful patient, making as little fuss as possible for those looking after him and never complaining. "I can do less and less things," he told me once, "but the lucky thing is that I still enjoy those things."

No less worthy of respect, my uncle Bill, as a Japanese prisoner after the fall of Hong Kong, did all that could be done for his fellows who appointed him as their liaison with the guards and other captors. He and his wife were generally credited with having done everything possible to alleviate the general misery.

I thought of these two men one weekend when my wife, Adele, and I were visiting her grandmother on Long Island, and I happened to overhear a conversation between her uncle, Douglas Burden, and his elderly mother, Adele Sloane Burden, who was, at the time, more often referred to as Mrs. Richard Tobin. During the talk, Douglas urged her to persuade his brother Jimmy not to play golf at the Piping Rock Club on the north shore of Long Island. Jimmy's game, it seems, was a disgrace to the family, at least as far as Douglas was concerned. Neither his mother nor my uncle would have gone along with this; they were much too kind to have hurt anyone's feelings for such a reason, but they would have sympathized with Douglas's distaste for any public display of athletic incompetence.

For a time it seemed my sister Priscilla might be deprived of many of life's great satisfactions. This shy and affectionate girl suffered from an even worse case of the depressive condition that plagued my father.

She and I had adjoining bedrooms on the fourth floor front of the family brownstone on Ninety-first Street. She, being my elder by almost two years, of course occupied the larger room with two windows on the street while I was relegated to the much smaller which had only one. I resented this. The bathroom in the middle of the fourth floor we shared, and I was disgusted at the time she took in it behind a door she always primly locked.

I was then enrolled at Bovee and she in Miss Chapin's, a few blocks south. Maggie, our nurse, would pick me up at noon and walk me down to Miss Chapin's to get Priscilla. My poor sister, at twelve, was undergoing the severe mental stress of a constant bad conscience over trivial matters. This was all part of her condition.

Such things were never discussed in those days. People were too apt to jump to conclusions that far exceeded the actual condition. When the doctors treating my father sought to trace the origin of his disease in his family, I kept my sharp little ears open and picked up the legend that, as a Newport debutante, grandmother Auchincloss had tried to drown herself (a tale barely creditable and utterly hushed up) and that a crazy niece of hers had actually murdered a woman friend.

Although I concealed my finds from the outside world, I was enchanted by such accounts, which made a dull family exciting. Despite the stern parental warnings, I told all my little friends that the doctors were probably going to put my sister in a straightjacket. My poor bewildered parents couldn't imagine where these rumors were coming from.

My unhappy sister would awake me at night with complaints like: "We were playing tag in the yard at recess today, and I touched a girl on the shoulder and cried 'You're it!' But did I actually touch her? Might I have cheated?"

You can imagine how much consolation she got from a kid brother angry at being awakened. Besides, I was already convinced that she got too much sympathy from our parents, whose growing alarm over her condition was, of course, not understandable to me. A crisis arose one Christmas when she refused to open a single present marked "For Priscilla," insisting that it might be for Mother, whose namesake she was.

My sister had a series of female paid companions who were disguised professionals trained to cheer her up and help her to find life interesting. They became, of course, a feature of family life not wholly welcome. I recall one who tried to stimulate conversation at breakfast by asking my father, a devoted Wagnerian, if he did not find the music of *Tristan* vulgar and sensuous. Another one, a rather pretty Miss Jack, was engaged to a man called Bill, and I used to infuriate her by singing excerpts from the song "My Bill," which Helen Morgan had then made famous in *Show Boat:* "He's just my Bill, an ordinary man; you'd meet him on the street and never notice him." Finally she actually gave notice, and Mother thought it was so silly she never scolded me.

The companion who was with us longest, a Miss Warfield, was an amiable, well-meaning, but thickly sentimental woman who was rumored in later years to have been some kin to the duchess of Windsor whom she certainly did not resemble. It was her enthusiastic theory that Priscilla be introduced to "Mother Nature" by spending a night outside in the woods in Maine. Great preparations were made under Miss Warfield's detailed instructions. Sheets, blankets, pillows, pots and pans, breakfast foods, insect deterrents, medicines, flashlights, and Lord knows what else were hauled by our reluctant chauffeur into the woods adjoining our property, and something like a camp was set up.

In the morning after a sleepless night the chauffeur and Maggie brought the adventurers back to the house, where they gratefully spent the day in bed.

Expert and expensive psychiatric treatment in those days was centered in Stockbridge, Massachusetts, and Priscilla was placed in the care of a famous and fashionable doctor there.

His treatment would, I am sure, be considered odd today. He opined that Priscilla's trouble originated in a family with three boys and she must be reintegrated in one with two girls and a doctor. Guess which doctor and guess his fee! Twenty thousand dollars a year, in the 1930s! But Mother believed in doctors and even in their fees. The money was paid and Priscilla moved to Stockbridge for a year or more. When she came home, she was just the same so far as I could see, but always in the company of a disguised trained nurse.

Mother, however, was by no means always to be put upon. She and I were once in Grand Central Station waiting for a train to take us to Stockbridge to spend a weekend with Priscilla, when whom should we see but our famous doctor, who had just detrained?

"Oh, Mrs. Auchincloss, I'm glad to run into you. I've had an emergency call and can't be with you this weekend as planned. But you'll find everything ready for you."

To my amazement I heard Mother's firm reply. "No, Doctor, that won't do. I'm afraid you'll have to take the train back to Stockbridge with me."

And he did! She was supporting him.

Mother did not hesitate to draft the family into her different projects for Priscilla. The family came first, and if one was ailing the others had to defer. Thus when Priscilla, behind as usual in her schoolwork, needed summer tutoring and Mother feared the effect on her of strange teachers, she induced my older brother to give up a trip to Europe to do the job.

John was something of a saint, always obliging her, but I was different. When Mother asked me to have Priscilla as my guest at the annual school dance at Groton, I flatly refused. Whereas John, at party after party, refrained from dancing that he might be free to rescue Priscilla when she was "stuck" too long with some frustrated youth.

She was not insensitive nor, by nature, ungrateful, but she never quite realized how much John did for her in these early days. People, even well brought up and thoughtful young women, are rarely inclined to acknowledge those who cover their disadvantages. Priscilla went her own way until the night (I shall never forget it!) when, one might say, she woke up. Her relief from illness must have been gradually arriving, but it was at a club dance where we spotted her, suddenly moving animatedly over the floor with a handsome young man I had never seen before. Both were smiling. I asked John if he had introduced them, and he said no, the man had just cut in. Although I have no intention of trivializing her condition or minimizing the difficulties of alleviating it, it seemed that Priscilla had, that very night, suddenly decided that life might be different. From then on she got better and better, and acquired all the friends she needed. She married happily and had three fine children. There were always to be bad times— severe recurrent depressions—but there were good ones as well.

I have not mentioned my brother Howland as he is still living and can still speak of his experience for himself. I honor him with silence, as I have tried to recapture our siblings, their struggles and kindnesses, with understanding and fairness.

We were united all of us in our family, but rarely deeply intimate. In the times of which I speak it seems there was more not discussed than otherwise. What was there, after all, to share at length, even among family? Loyalty and consideration—this is how it was among brothers and sisters in the world from which we came: society, as it was known, mostly by those who found themselves admiring its surfaces from the outskirts. Those of us on the inside, feeling the expectations and demands, may have felt somewhat differently. At least on occasion.

3

What Some Call "Society"

THERE IS NO such thing as a predominating and generally recognized Society in New York City today, but there are, indeed, many societies. The so-called Social Register has swollen to the size of a fat telephone directory, and it is just as common for people to refuse to be listed as to seek to get in. The announcement of engagements and marriages in the Sunday *New York Times* lists dozens of couples. In my youth, the social page of the daily *Times* devoted its left-hand column to a single pair with a large portrait of the bride or fiancée who were apt to be known, or at least known of, by a good portion of the readers.

In the 1920s and '30s there existed indubitably, however hard to define, a social structure called "society" that regarded itself as just that. These persons resided on the East Side of Manhattan (never west except below Fifty-ninth Street) as far south as Union Square and as far north as Ninety-sixth Street. The members (if that is the word; it doesn't seem quite right) were largely Protestants of Anglo-Saxon origin. (Note that Catholics and nonpracticing Jews were not always excluded if rich enough.) The men were apt to be in business, finance, or law, sometimes in medicine, rarely in the church and almost never in politics. Franklin Roosevelt was an exception and not a popular one, either.

For the women, society offered a certain power and prestige, but it also tended to reinforce conventions that limited those with ambition. I had known Janet Auchincloss's daughter, Jackie Bouvier, since her mother's marriage to Father's first cousin Hugh D. Auchincloss. But they lived in Washington and Jackie was a good bit younger than I, so I saw her rarely. We all, of course, were drawn by her charm and beauty, but such qualities are not unusual, and none of us predicted her remarkable destiny. I did, however, have a curious premonition of it.

I was spending a weekend with my brother John in Washington, and he and his wife had asked the Hugh D. Auchinclosses and Jackie for a family dinner. During the meal we learned that Jackie was engaged to a New Yorker called Husted. After the meal she and I sat in the corner, and I quizzed her about him. I had just published a novel titled *Sybil* about a rather dull girl, which Jackie, perhaps surprisingly, had read.

"Oh, you've written my life," she told me. "Sybil Bouvier, Sybil Husted. Respectable, middle-class, moderately well off. Accepted everywhere. Decent and dull."

And then a curious but strong feeling gripped me, quite unlike anything that usually accompanied parlor chatter. *Why was this pretty girl talking such nonsense? Didn't she know that a very different fate awaited her?* A week later we learned the engagement was off. So sometimes women did break the rules and found that it worked out quite successfully.

The real and formidable influence of society was, fittingly, social. Those inside society's ranks controlled the private schools, the clubs, the country clubs, the subscription dances for the young, the Episcopal and Presbyterian churches, as well as the larger banks and law firms. It is commonly said that they have been relegated to the past. That is not so. They have simply lost their monopoly; they have had to move over and share their once closely guarded powers with the new rich, who are quite willing to spare the older generation so long as they are allowed to copy, and perhaps enhance, their style. See any Ralph Lauren ad.

My eight great-grandparents were all natives of Manhattan and all uncritical members of the society I have attempted to describe. As they had multiple siblings and numberless descendants, the city seemed awash with cousins, and I was apt to be surprised if I didn't find one or more in any circle I attended. To me, New York society (we never used the term) was not a class that dominated my world; it simply was that world. It was said of a school that I later attended, Groton, that there was no snobbishness because the boys all came from the same background, and there was actually some truth to this.

The four principal families of my origin seem to merge together in retrospect into a single unit: an uninspiring but decent and respectable bourgeois tribe. Yet how different they seemed to a growing and observant boy! Father's mother's family, the Russells of New York and simpler pre-Vanderbilt Newport, had been rich from imports and clipper ships prior to the Civil War and prominent in the society described in the diary of Mayor Philip Hone, a cousin. But all was now in the past. Despite their Italian villas and marble busts taken on Roman honeymoons, the Russells, by the time of my childhood, were faintly shabby.

Much smarter and up to date were Mother's maternal family, the Dixons, a cheerful, close-knit, handsome, and worldly group who set a high but not unreasonable value on appearance in clothes, sport, and general behavior. They were devoted to each other, and their neighboring brownstones on Forty-ninth Street were known as Dixon Alley. But at parties they were less inclined to cluster; they mingled and didn't interfere with family unless a girl was stuck on the dance floor or a boy was spending too much time at the bar.

The Auchinclosses were the Johnny-come-latelies, not bringing their woolen business from Scotland until 1803. The first Hugh Auchincloss was interned as an enemy alien in the War of 1812 and unsprung by an indignant visit by his wife to President Madison. (Anyone could go to the White House then.) The family produced a high percentage of vigorous males who made their rapid, unopposed entry into society through business and legal aptitude as well as advantageous marriages. The dour Scotch ways were soon abandoned, though I can remember a maiden great aunt who, during a visit to Bar Harbor, refused to go with us to the swimming club because men and women shared the pool. And that was when women's bathing suits covered them from neck to toe with long, black stockings added!

The Stantons, Mother's father's clan, were too few in number for notice, except for the elegant Uncle Ed, who sent his shirts to Europe to be properly laundered and was so esteemed by his rich friends that they eased him into a job for which he had little qualification: nothing less than general manager of the Metropolitan Opera. His unexpected passion for German opera when the boxholders all preferred the Italian led to his dismissal, and he died abroad of alcoholism.

New York, unlike Boston, had, even in my young days, scant respect for genealogy. Although some of the Auchincloss wives had distinguished colonial forebears (my great-grandmother Auchincloss could boast that both her grandmothers were Saltonstalls), I doubt that had much to do with the family's rise. But an early origin—when combined with a large fortune— will attract a certain awe in the city. To be an Astor or a Rockefeller was to be important even to the oldest New Yorker.

I remember as a boy Mr. and Mrs. John D. Jr., who summered in Seal Harbor, Maine, visiting the neighboring Bar Harbor Swimming Club. Received like royalty, they passed, nodding graciously, through the umbrella tables on the club lawn where members were having a noontime drink. Mr. Rockefeller was not a noticeable figure, but his wife, who had put the family on the social map and also orchestrated the splendid landscape architecture of their great estate in Tarrytown had a wonderful, almost Edwardian, elegance.

It was she, notoriously, who had made a philanthropist of her spouse. Yet he had refused to support her in her major interest: the Museum of Modern Art, which he regarded as red and radical. This was a problem in the museum's early years, for although Mrs. Rockefeller had money of her own, it was not nearly on the same scale as her husband's. If she gave only, say, $50,000 where a million was expected, too many of the wealthy would also reduce their pledges. Peggy, the wife of David Rockefeller, downplayed any tensions. "My father-in-law," she claimed, "so adored his wife that he couldn't bear to have her not share all his interests." Eager to hear more, I couldn't help pointing out that this wasn't so much love as possession. After this comment, little more was divulged. (Of course the Rockefeller children ultimately followed their mother and became the principal supporters of the museum.)

While on the subject of such prominent families we must, of course, raise the name of the Vanderbilts, who dominated newspaper accounts of society. But this was not enough to ensure widespread admiration: The dynasty's rather too-palatial residences tainted them with vulgarity to a discriminating minority. Edith Wharton spoke of the family as engaged in a constant Battle of Thermopylae against bad taste, which they never won.

Revered by all in my boyhood for rectitude and the highest financial responsibility were the partners of the House of

Morgan. To my young and naïve ears they might have been the twelve apostles. I should note here that my father's law firm represented J. P. Morgan & Co. and that my mother's father had been head of a small trust company that was part of the Morgan empire. As a little girl she had been staying in a summer hotel in Bar Harbor, Maine, when the great Morgan yacht, the *Corsair*, had steamed in, and an invitation to dine onboard sent to the Stantons, who promptly accepted, though they had another engagement. A fictitious cold was used as an excuse to their previous host when the date was cancelled. When Mother, overhearing all this on the telephone, protested, she was simply told: "When you're older, dear, you'll understand these things."

The kind of dissipation of large fortunes in gambling and women that forms such a staple for novelists of nineteenth-century French fiction was never a characteristic of American society, even in the South, though it certainly existed, and made a kind of surreptitious appearance in the New York of the 1880s and '90s. Certainly by the time of my father's generation (he was born in 1886), the sacredness of capital was an established creed, and even the Vanderbilts (George of Biltmore always excepted) probably lived within their incomes. The work ethic applied to all. My father had two brothers-in-law born wealthy men who lost the bulk of their fortunes by insisting on managing their money themselves rather than leaving it to professionals. "Had they been beachcombers," Father used to say, "they'd be rich men today."

I can't think of a single example among my contemporary

friends and relations who dissipated a substantial inheritance. Many vastly increased them. Some parents were ingenious in training their offspring in the care and management of money. The Rockefellers are perhaps the extreme example of a family whose members were successfully taught financial responsibility from an early age.

The father of my friend Bill Scranton, former governor of Pennsylvania, gave Bill, when we were at Yale, a much larger allowance than other students. But with it went the responsibility for two poor relatives who would presumably be destitute if Bill blew it all. Even bribes in the family, theoretically meretricious, sometimes worked. I know of a case where an idle youth with bad marks was turned into a star by the lure of a glittering motorcycle. He went on to become a Wall Street magnate.

A common objection to inherited wealth is that it stifles the urge to work. I have not generally observed this to be true, except in cases where the individual involved would probably not have achieved very much had he toiled in the vineyard. My richest friend and contemporary, Marshall Field IV, whom I met in law school, is sometimes cited as a victim of wealth; he succumbed at age fifty to drugs. But his nervous troubles were a matter of tragic inheritance; the story of the Fields is like that of the House of Atreus.

I pause for a moment with Marshall. The first thirty years of his life were wonderful ones. He seemed blessed of the gods. He had looks, brains, health, charm, a lovely and loving wife, a devoted family, many interesting and lively friends, and pots of gold. At Virginia Law School, where he and I were classmates, he was Notes editor of the Law Review and president of the law school and of the university's honor court. The honor system was sacred at Virginia: the most honorable of the students, and they were fine men indeed, would not hesitate to turn in their best friends for cheating. I remember watching Marshall preside at a session of the court when the mother of the defendant rose and screamed, "Are you, Marshall Field, son of one of the richest men in this country, going to disgrace my poor boy for life by throwing him out of this university?"

When Marshall joined me later he was mopping his brow. "There's got to be an easier way to make a living," he muttered.

In the war he served creditably as an officer aboard an aircraft carrier and in peace untangled the snarl of his father's newspapers, until the Field darkness that had caused his grandfather's suicide and other family tragedies descended upon him.

I draw the curtain.

4

A Few Words About Women

OF COURSE, like most men I judged women by my mother. As the wife of a prosperous lawyer, she had two nurses to care for four minor children, a cook for her meals, a waitress to serve them, a chambermaid to clean the house, and a chauffeur to drive her. Her days were thus free for some not very taxing charity work, lunches with friends at her club, matinees or concerts, visits to museums.

If a woman were intellectually ambitious, which my mother was, she could take courses at Columbia or the New School. In the hot months, when we moved from town to the country and I was sometimes taken to meet my commuter father on his evening train, I contrasted the sweating cheek that he gave me to kiss with the cool one of Mother's beside the swimming pool. Why was it so great to be a man?

At my day school in the city I had a friend whose family sent him to classes in a red Rolls-Royce limousine that I greatly envied. I did not much ingratiate myself with Mother when I asked her, "If you went downtown to work like Daddy, do you think that between you, you could make enough money so we could have a red Rolls-Royce?"

Why should one rest while the other toiled? I didn't get it.

It was commonly said that because so many women were possessed of great wealth in their own right, that they exercised considerable economic power. It is truer to say that they could have. But all that was left by tacit consent to the men. Women, before they took jobs in the professions, were content with the power they exercised in the home, where they ran the household and the children, selected the life style and the friends, chose the vacation spots and the charities to be supported and even the church to be attended. The problems of finance and moneymaking they didn't even want to hear about. Their attitude was summed up by this bit of dialogue between husband and wife from T. S. Eliot's *The Cocktail Party*.

> LAVINIA: It's only that I have a more practical mind.
> EDWARD: Only because you've told me so often. I'd like to see *you* filling up an income-tax form.
> LAVINIA: Don't be silly, Edward. When I say practical, I mean practical in the things that really matter.

Men accepted this division eagerly, thinking that they had won, as did women, with more reason. If a woman made her own fortune, except in a conceded territory as the stage or cosmetics, men called her a witch, like Hetty Green. Women didn't care what Hetty Green was called, and they were right. It didn't matter.

* * *

Mother's woman friends were mostly in their early fifties when an old Groton classmate of mine remarked of one of them (whom I shall call Rosette) crudely but interestingly, that she alone of the group remembered that she was still a woman. I was rather taken aback, but, thinking it over, I began to see what he meant. Rosette had a bit of French blood, and she made the most of it. Her eyes, her gestures, her tone of voice in the presence of men showed not only her awareness of their difference but her pleasure in it. I do not in the least mean that she was provocative or flirty; it was to imply that to her the fact that the sexes had a reason for being differently constructed was always in the picture.

Did that mean that males had to be catered to? *Never.* French women are absolute rulers in their own domain. But what did my Groton friend think of the rest of Mother's friends? That they were unattractive, unappealing? Certainly not. He only meant that, to them, the game of sex was over. They had attained what they had wanted: in most cases, a husband, often successful and frequently faithful, and children, largely by this time adult and usually good enough citizens. To describe these ladies: they inclined to be large and strongly built, rarely stout, well dressed but not too stylish, accustomed to deference from those who served them, and with good formal manners that placed their interlocutor on an exact par with themselves, if not sometimes a trifle lower.

They left all business matters entirely to their husbands, assuming that everything that went on "downtown" was as strictly honorable as in their own pure lives. They ran their sometimes large households with commendable efficiency and sat conscientiously on meritorious charitable boards. They had a good deal of free time in which to visit each other, to read, to go to the theatre, to hear music, to play cards, to visit museums. Most of them were more cultivated and interesting than their husbands, but they all were aware that their lot in life was easier than that of most of their fellow men and were not inclined to rock boats. They would have been angered to be called snobs.

They wore little jewelry but what they did was very good. Mrs. Clarance Pell, whose husband was the longtime president of the Racquet Club, wore a jangling bracelet of small gold racquets, each representing one of his championships. My mother used to say it was the envy of every social climber in New York.

The lady I have called Rosette, an excellent housekeeper, was twice widowed and used to boast: "Well, at least I have made two men very comfortable." I doubt you would have heard such a remark from Mother's other friends. To them the husband was merged in the family; the children got equal attention. Mother, who had a way of carrying domestic concerns to extremes, went so far as to assert, hearing of F.D.R.'s polio: "Eleanor must have been glad it wasn't one of the children." But that was just Mother.

None of Mother's friends had jobs, but there were some like Mrs. Alsop, who were very active in politics, or Ruth Draper, who triumphed on the stage. I liked how one of them defined the words "My rod and staff": "My rod is my church and my staff is my money." Frances Perkins, the first woman to hold a post in a President's cabinet, was known to some of them and admired by all. But she was not an intimate, though she belonged to a tightly knit ladies' discussion group of which Mother was a leading member. F.D.R. at a cabinet meeting was known to have thrown this smiling question to his secretary of labor: "What will they think of *that*, Frances, in the Junior Fortnightly?"

Suppose a lady of this order did not find a husband or did not choose to have one. Well, if she happened to be an heiress, it didn't matter. A Frenchman visiting New York was supposed to have observed that it couldn't harbor a really worldly society because it contained so many rich old maids who in Paris would have been married by force. And indeed, he had quite a list: the Misses Anne Morgan, Ruth Twombly, Julia Berwind, Anne Jennings, Helen Frick, Edith and Maud Wetmore. Less richly endowed but still independent virgins might lead social lives not dissimilar to that of their married friends, depending for affection on loving nephews and nieces, but if really poor they were doomed to act as companions to ancient and long-surviving parents. Indeed, this latter was often considered their sacred duty, even where funds existed for a paid companion.

Suppose the lonely female, even if well to do, was—hush, hush—a lesbian? The term was little used; a preferable one was "horsey." Such matters were better locked in the closet. The particular one in our lives I shall call Aunt Daisy, though she was not related, but a dear friend of the family. She was a large, imposing woman, hefty rather than stout, with blond hair drawn straight over her scalp to knot in back. She wore

mannish suits and her love life was hidden but far from un-
guessable. What she believed in was almost the exact opposite
of everything Mother stood for: that life could, and perhaps
should, be lived for the appreciation of art, if one did not have
the good luck to have been born an artist oneself.

Mother was fond of Aunt Daisy, but she never yielded an inch
in her conviction that the only really good life was to have a
faithful husband enthusiastically at work in a beloved profession and a faithful wife happily raising a large and essentially
obedient family. The amazing thing about my mother was that
she was always able to see her own case as a thing apart, having no special relation to others, so that she brought a fresh
and unbiased mind of penetrating power to the problems of
her friends who sought her advice in droves. As one of them,
whose happy marriage she arranged in a difficult situation,
told me, "I was lucky not to be related to your mother, for her
mind doesn't work as well with her own family."

Aunt Daisy could only pity Mother for what she regarded as
philistine principles. Daisy boasted of having heard more than
fifty performances of *Tristan* at the opera house and rarely left
town for fear of missing a cultural event. "If you see a tree,
give it a kick for me," she used to say to those departing in rus-
tic retreat. She lived amid the large and handsome objects of
her prosperous and utterly respectable family, whose money
came from one of Commodore Vanderbilt's corrupt judges.
New York had its compromises.

Aunt Daisy was warmly interested in any of her friends'

children who showed the least intellectual curiosity, and her talk of art in any form was witty and amusing. Her quotations, mostly of poetry, were wonderfully relevant to the subject under discussion; she was the first person to make me aware of pleasures that were of only tertiary importance to my parents.

But Aunt Daisy's tragedy was my bitter disillusionment. Her increasing alcoholism rendered her inanely sentimental about works of art, particularly music, about which she had formerly made good sense. In an opera box (one constantly loaned to her by a rich and devoted friend) she would ask me to bring her drinks from the bar and wax irate when I told her it wasn't allowed. The sad thing was that her deterioration struck me as a kind of justification of Mother's point of view. To this sorry state an overindulgence in the arts brought one!

The elderly husband of Aunt Daisy's most intimate friend once described Aunt Daisy to Mother as the "dark shadow" in his life. Did that mean she and his wife had an affair? I hope so.

A somewhat similar warning though in a different area was offered by a dazzlingly beautiful first cousin of Mother's whom I shall call Sally. Sally's looks and charm had made her a noted figure in society: she had been married twice—the second time happily though both times childlessly—to attractive men about town who shared her epicurean view of a life dedicated to pleasure and the maintenance of a fine appearance.

Like Aunt Daisy, but in a very different way, she was Mother's opposite, but as Mother's senior by a year, she had dominated her in childhood and the bond was never loosened.

Sally, whose closest next of kin was a brother married to a great heiress, had once proposed to leave her own not inconsiderable estate to Mother's children, but had been dissuaded by Mother, who had insisted on the brother's preference. It was a typical example of what I used to call Mother's "magnificent disloyalty."

Sally's end might have pointed to the moral in a story written by Mother had she written any. Living alone in an apartment hotel as a widow, surrounded by great gaping dolls in wonderful dresses, she took to the bottle and eventually threw herself out the window. A news account described a pillow in her apartment bearing the legend: "Don't worry—it never happens."

The problem that brought these ladies to the grave was, of course, simply alcoholism, but my young, family-influenced mind insisted on the moral lesson. But there was a third woman in my life who also died of drink and who also lived in striking disaccord with Mother's principles. About her, my mother and I did not ultimately agree. This was Elsa Stanton, wife of Mother's much younger brother, Bill, and the only human being I think Mother actually hated. I'm afraid she was most unjust.

Bill Stanton, a charming fellow, early orphaned by the premature demise of my maternal grandparents, had emigrated in his twenties to Hong Kong where he could afford, with thirty ponies and the needed houseboys, to lead a life based in polo that he couldn't possibly have afforded in New York. There in due time he had met a merry, plump, twice-married but now free, charming lady, a brilliant figure in the crown colony's smart international society, some dozen years his senior with two grown children. He fell violently in love with her, a passion that never cooled, and they were married, very happily. But to Mother, who had been a kind of substitute parent to this adored younger brother, the fact that Elsa could give him no children, was older, and drank, made the marriage a travesty that she could never forgive.

The rest of the family appreciated Elsa's high spirits, humor, and devotion to Bill. She also had great courage, which appeared when Hong Kong fell to the Japanese, and she and Bill were interned in Stanley Prison. Joseph Alsop, a fellow prisoner, speaks in his memoirs of the great example in sheer guts that Elsa provided to the other inmates. Her leg had been broken during the siege, but she saved her diamonds from the guards by secreting them in her cast.

One Japanese officer, with the strange politeness that they sometimes (too rarely) showed their victims, called on Elsa in her cell to ask if they could use her house as an officers club. She wanted to know why they bothered to ask.

"Because it's so much nicer to have permission," he explained.

"Well, you *don't* have permission!" she declared.

Needless to say, she found the house gutted when they returned after the war.

Mother's hostility to Elsa (which incidentally was thoroughly returned) lasted unremittingly until the latter's death from drink. It was quite unlike Mother. Even when she had to search among the family jewels for an appropriate wedding present for Elsa she manifested a sentiment that could only be called savage. Like a true puritan she selected the most valuable jewel of all, a diamond choker with a huge pin, and said she hoped Elsa would stick it right through her jugular vein!

The columnist Joseph Alsop described Elsa in his memoirs, quite erroneously, as the richest woman in Hong Kong. At her death he said to me, "I suppose Elsa's fortune will be tied up for the children. What will your uncle live on?" A typical Joe question. I replied, "He will live on what he has always lived on: his own income. Elsa left him everything she had, and he has already settled it on her children."

Part II

Education and After

◇◇◇

5

Teachers, Beloved and Otherwise

BOVEE WAS A PRIVATE day school for boys from six to the age of twelve when they were apt to be sent off to boarding school. It occupied a tall brown stone building on Fifth Avenue opposite the Central Park Zoo, through which we were marched two by two at recess but not allowed to visit. That we could do on weekends with parents or nurses if we were not taken to a country estate.

Our building rose to six stories with a class to each floor in order of age, so that the boys who climbed to the top were presumably the oldest and strongest. The school, which expired in 1929, was still in its heyday when I entered. In 1923 it remained under the able administration of its vigorous founder and owner, Miss Kate Bovee, and it was an admired institution considered to be quite the equal of Buckley and St. Bernard's. But unlike these noteworthy institutions, Bovee did not share the fashionable anti-Semitism of that day; it admitted Jewish boys, many of them from "our crowd" and drawn from the great German Jewish finance families of the city. Also in tow were the sons of New York's literary and artistic circles, who were suspiciously regarded by most of our watchful parents.

The young Efrem Zimbalist Jr. and Mel Ferrer, both destined to become actors, were in my class. This did not effect the school's social position; Jack Astor, who would grow up to be Jack Astor, was sent there as well.

Kate Bovee was not a woman to be trifled with; she was even known to hurl books at recalcitrant boys. There was an aggressive note in the school cheer: "Rah, Rah, Rah, Ree, Ree, Ree; Bee o Vee double E Bovee!"

But all this came to a sorry end when Miss Kate died prematurely, leaving the establishment to her not so serious and rather fatuous younger sister, Eleanor. This was a woman known to have demanded of a class supposed to be studying in silence, "Who is talking in this room?"

"You are!," came the shouts in response.

Before her arrival at Bovee, Eleanor had been teaching eloquence to the girls at Miss Spence's. Gretchen Finletter has well described this ambitious instructor at work there in a delightful memoir: "Miss Bovee explained the 'one, two, three.' This meant that before the great line of the poem (she was reciting) the pupil was to pause and count 'one, two, three,' and then give it everything."

Thus in Emerson's poem about the squirrel and the mountain, the pupil must render the squirrel's retort to the mountain's taunting of his smallness as follows:

> *If I cannot carry forests on my back,*
> *Neither can you [one, two, three, twinkle, dimple,*
> *and with great archness] crack a nut!*

I don't have to tell more than one other thing about Miss Eleanor to explain the school's collapse under her guidance. She instituted a Noble Life medal for the boy who had led the noblest life in the year involved. Of course she was conned into giving it to the boy who we all knew had the dirtiest tongue in the school! And what her insistence on pronouncing her surname and the school's in the French manner (Beauvais) did to our school cheer can be imagined.

Things went from bad to worse until Miss Eleanor decided to give up teaching and move to her beloved France. But she had the last word, for she sold the building to her advantage and threw the poor faculty out of work just as the Great Depression of 1929 hit.

They were not at all a bad faculty; with decent management they could have contributed to what certainly could have been an effective school. The Latin teacher, Mr. Van Wormer, a huge stentorian man, conveyed some of the authority of ancient Rome, and Mr. Sedgwick, small and precise, appeared a fitting teacher of mathematics. The school seems to have limited them in terms of disciplinary tactics to hair pulling: Van Wormer would grab a handful and shake a boy; Sedgwick would take a strand and twist it painfully.

French was the department of two elderly Gallic maiden sisters, one a timid white-haired creature known simply as Mademoiselle and the other, bony and dominating, who was called the real Mademoiselle. She would stand at the head of her stairway in the midst of the morning rush crying *Doucement!* which the boys mocked as "Do some more."

It was the custom to give the teachers something at Christmas, a tradition of which Mother heartily disapproved. I could only get stockings from her for the women educators. These less than luxurious presents were quite obviously scorned by the real Mademoiselle who, after the slenderest of acknowledgments, held up before the class an envelope given her by a luckier boy crying: "I can feel it contains a five-dollar gold piece like last year." When I told Mother this I couldn't even get stockings out of her the next year.

The poor mademoiselles, when out of work like the others, tried to start a dress shop with a rather limited selection of only eight dresses. My parents, of course, were not unaware of the school's decline, and wanted to transfer me to St. Bernard's, despite the colorful picture in its front hall of Lucrezia Borgia presiding over a conclave of the college of cardinals during the pontificate of her father, Alexander VI. But I liked Bovee and its lax discipline and my few silly friends there. Life was not taken too seriously, even where sports were concerned. This, I realized, was remarkable in a world over-stimulated by athleticism, not to mention competition.

I recall a new boy who affected the "mucker pose" arriving in time for baseball in the park and asking, "Where's de coach?" Someone pointed to a Fifth Avenue bus rumbling by. "Dere's de coach."

Tommy Curtis, my particular pal, was almost a reason in himself to take a boy out of Bovee. Though in my class and presumably more or less the same age, he was three years my senior. Furthermore, he affected a high sophistication and was always talking about Broadway musicals named *Gay Paree* or *The Countess Maritza*. In later life he lived in Paris, reviewed movies, and wrote a biography of Erich von Stroheim. One summer he penned a letter urging me to read the current best-seller *The Well of Loneliness*, an early novel about lesbianism. Mother, who never hesitated to open her children's mail, handed me this epistle as if with tongs, saying, "I don't like your friend Curtis." She must have not read *The Well of Loneliness*, or the letter would not have been given to me at all. I was eleven!

Tommy added to his sins in Mother's eye by living on the despised West side and being sent to school by his widowed mother in the aforementioned red Rolls-Royce limousine. I remember being mystified when I overheard Mother asking Father, "Do you suppose there ever *was* a Mister Curtis?"

Anyway, despite my correspondents and their seemingly controversial subjects, my parents let me remain at Bovee. I had only another year there before being sent to Groton, where my status as a graduate's son meant automatic admission, whatever school I had been to before. But I have sometimes wondered if I was sent to the Knickerbocker Greys as a sort of disinfectant following the contamination infected by Tommy Curtis and other Bovee miscreants.

The Greys were a military institution run in the Park Avenue armory and designed for boys largely taken from nearby private day schools. Two afternoons a week we were marched to the armory for training in close order drills and the handling of fake firearms. Uniforms were provided; mock battles planned; and the officers, much envied, wore plumes in their caps. My Fowler first cousins were among the latter, but I remained a humble private during my entire year there. I didn't, however, mind the place after I had finally persuaded Mother that it didn't become a soldier to be accompanied to the Greys by a nursemaid.

My enrollment was supposedly voluntary, but it actually stemmed from a remark of mine taken by my parents as cute. Asked if I would like to go to the Greys, I replied that I should certainly be prepared in the event of another war. I was too young to remember the First World War, though I was actually a baby in an army camp in Kentucky when it ended. Father was in an officers' training camp at the time, and Mother, with three children at that point and four maids, had joined him there. Mocked for this number of domestics in later years, she simply said: "Martha Whitney had taken eight."

The armistice saved Father from the trenches, but two uncles and innumerable cousins had gone, and the talk I heard of the conflict engraved early on in my mind the apprehension that enlistment might be the direful and unavoidable fate of every generation. But the Greys nonetheless struck me as a harmless and even amusing facsimile of world carnage. Once I got the hang of it, it was rather fun to march in unison about that gigantic hall to the shouts "Squad right!" or "Right by squadrons!" or "Squad left!" or "Left by squadrons!" In mock battle, where one was instructed to indicate that one was a casualty simply by lying down, I thought I should add a touch of drama by clutching my heart and reeling to the floor.

This was followed by the reproof of a plumed cousin. Of course it was all play-acting seemingly frivolous when considered against the dark future of boarding school, which loomed like a black cloud on the immediate horizon. People would tell me, "You're just going to love Groton," but I didn't think they believed it themselves. And why did my older brother never warn me about it? It was, I thought, all part of a conspiracy as to how the world, the real world, was made to seem bearable to those about to enter it.

If the Greys were a kind of benign microcosm of war, dancing school on Thursday afternoons in the ballroom of the Colony Club might be said to have been a similarly junior form of adult entertainment. Older people danced, yes, but certainly none I had seen in my limited travels moved in a fashion anywhere near what we were encouraged to adopt. Perhaps, though this was unlikely, none I knew had suffered under the dictatorship to minuet offered up by Mrs. Hubbell, a stiff, solid, silkily barked oak tree of a woman who was reputed to have instructed the princess royal of Britain in the art of Terpsichore.

Awesome it was for a boy to be selected by that figure of robust carriage to be her partner in the demonstration of a step. Without fail one would be instructed, rather vigorously, to press a hand more firmly on that unslender, thickly corseted back. Could any male have ever clasped it in love? Perhaps not, though in a thunderous gale it might have offered safe and ample harbor. What a man Mr. Hubbell must have been! Never shall I forget how our venerable instructress, determined that her pupils be not behind in the latest craze, slowly and gravely bent her knees to illustrate the dip of the Charleston.

But soon all commotion would end. All such activity was swept away by boarding school and Groton. When the sexes next met, it was in black pumps and formal dresses, in the uneasy shyness of the junior subscription dance, where, as one girl put it, even the ladies' room stank of fear. The battles of society start young.

6

My Life in Crime

I WAS NINE YEARS OLD when I began a silent but rather dangerous form of what I suppose was rebellion. Or perhaps mere but short-lived insanity. I committed a series of larcenies. I had never stolen before and would, save for this brief interlude, never do so again. It was all quite curious, even to myself. It began with toys. The children of the summer people on Breezy Way in Lawrence, Long Island, with whom I played, had ample toys, and it was a simple matter for me, on occasion, to possess myself surreptitiously of an item coveted. But crime, like vermin, has the tendency toward rapid swelling, and I soon came to desire items of greater significance, including, alas, those belonging to adults. The most valuable of these that I can first recall was a pocket comb in a gold slipcase which I took from the bureau of a family weekend guest. Its loss was not discovered. And the streak continued.

What were my feelings? Not ones of severe guilt, anyway. I knew of course that theft was wrong, even rather importantly wrong. But it didn't have any real existence to my twisted reckoning unless it was discovered; concealed it was nothing. Not the slightest communication could be risked, however, even with Tommy Curtis or Rivington Pyne, my two best and perhaps most similarly adventurous friends at Bovee. The precarious feeling of the adventure was entirely conditional; everything depended on my silence. And then, not long after the epoch-making theft of the comb, I was smitten with a new kind of violent temptation, far stronger than any I had felt for the rather junky items I had so far acquired and carefully hidden away.

Uncle Russell Auchincloss, Father's very dignified and awesome older brother, was spending a weekend with us in Lawrence, and he unwisely showed me a golden gadget on his watch chain from which you could pull a scissors, a nail file, and God knows what else. I was seized with a longing for it. It had to be mine. Going to his bedroom when he was playing tennis with Father, I found the gadget detached from its chain on the bureau, and I took it. Was I mad? How did I ever expect to get away with it? Nor did I. My uncle complained; everyone, maids and all, were questioned. The house was searched. Then came the denouement: Maggie discovered my cache and, of course, despite my pleas betrayed me to my mother.

The silence that followed was beyond chastening. At first, not a word was spoken to me, so I knew that the matter was too grave for immediate retribution. That came on Monday morning, when we were back in town, and my sister, Priscilla, and I were waiting in the front hall for Maggie to take us to school. Father, on his way to work, suddenly appeared, striding down the stairway, and addressed me in a loud stentorian voice that I had not heard before. He announced that if I were ever caught stealing again, I should be whipped. Then he charged out the front door.

I was appalled, but I sensed, even then, that this would never happen because I would never steal again. I didn't believe that Father even possessed a whip; he had never physically chastised me. I had no great sense of guilt or shame; theft was simply something that didn't work and had to be given up forever, and that was that. I don't think I could steal a loaf of bread today if I were starving. But there was a curious aftermath to the scene in the hallway.

It did not come on the part of my father. He never again mentioned this aspect of my life to me, nor did it seem to have made the slightest difference in his attitude toward me. Yet I have always strongly suspected that it had appalled him and that he had deliberately attempted to blot out of his mind the idea that a son of his could be a thief. It was simply not part of the world to which he lovingly aspired, the man's world of sports, clubs, finance. This was the realm of the noisy, numerous, neighboring, highly masculine Auchincloss cousins with whom, from childhood, he had been closely associated.

Later on in life, my father rather unexpectedly told me that, however little I shared what he considered the Auchincloss traits, which I had felt so sorely lacking, I had always been his favorite child. My siblings found him amiable but detached. They did not suspect the lonelier more sensitive side that he tended to hide, but which, perhaps because of my own temperament, I perceived and empathized with. My mother's understanding of this part of my father was what gave this all-loving wife her total power over him. To some extent I shared this with her; he was not ashamed to show me his fragility.

He was born a twin but had lost his twin brother at age two. A psychiatrist who later treated him opined that his emotional problems may have been engendered by his mother's violent grief over the loss of his brother, which might have given the survivor a false sense of guilt, but who knows? Father, through the Howland family, was a third cousin of F.D.R., whom he very faintly resembled. Without his occasional depressions he might have had a more important career as a corporate lawyer, but he did well enough.

The aftermath to the discovery of my theft, to which I have referred, should have come as no surprise to me. Mother asked me, reasonably and even gently, to bring her everything that I had stolen, and I proceeded to comply. But I didn't bring her them all. I feared that the whole list might disturb the air of pardon that was settling over the family. But I nonetheless felt it was my sacred duty to see that every item still withheld was returned, however secretly, to its rightful owner. Only thus could I assure myself that the whole horrid business had returned to the void in which I had originally conceived it.

The toys presented little problem. I simply added them, when unobserved, to the ravaged treasure troves of my young friends. "Oh, there it is," one of them might observe. "I was wondering where it had got to." But I was stuck with two objects: a small silver tray, shaped like a heart, with the initials C.P.D., which I knew stood for Courtland Palmer Dixon, a cousin and neighbor, parental visits to whom rarely included small and noisy boys, and a small child's drinking cup decorated with painted circles, taken from an infrequently patronized notions shop in nearby Cedarhurst, the village of our Long Island retreat. I cannot imagine what drew me to either one, but there they were, seemingly fatal hurdles to my recovered innocence.

I had to wait a long time before I had a chance to go to the Dixons. Mother was quite often a guest there, but when I asked if I might accompany her, the answer was usually "No, there's nothing for you to do there." But at last came the day when she took me along. There were Dixon cousins my age visiting and so I was included. Finally, there was the opportunity for my almost-complete restitution. There was joy in my heart as I slipped the little ashtray onto a table. Of course, it had never been missed.

The cup was another matter. And it would be the only article that would ultimately stand between myself and relief. Father commuted in summer, and I was sometimes taken to meet his train. What was my dismay to discover on one such evening that the building which had housed the fatal shop had been razed! When I got home I took the cursed cup into a grove of trees and smashed it into pieces, stamping on each shard until it was dust. And then I experienced a great lift of heart. I was free! Free forever!

* * *

Unfortunately there is more to disclose. Perhaps it should have come earlier, in sequence, but it slipped my mind before my previous confession unleashed it. Which, looking back, I find worrisome, the suggestion, which combined with the earlier benefits, of a kind of destructive nature. For you see, at a still earlier age, that of eight, I committed a much more serious crime: that of vandalism. Unlike my other excursion into crime, it was never discovered, and the event had neither precedent nor repetition in my whole life. It was unique and extraordinary. I cannot explain it by anything in my character or upbringing. But here it is.

For a summer in Bar Harbor, Maine, my parents had rented a house on the top of a large hill owned by a Dr. Thorndike, a rich and deeply respected old Bostonian who had built other houses on the hill for his married daughters. There had been, years before, a beloved daughter who had died young. A small, unfurnished structure where she had "played house" was preserved intact in her memory. No one ever entered it but the cleaning woman.

I broke into it, smashing every piece of china in the little place. Why this madness seized me I shall never know. Was there some sort of anger that I had not otherwise acknowledged? What on earth was I feeling? Afterward, I tried to forget it myself. I attempted to believe it had never happened, as there were no repercussions. I never went near the little house again; I began to think it had not occurred.

But it had, indeed. The repercussions for me occurred some forty years later. I was having Sunday lunch with my elderly parents when the discussion fell on a peculiarly nasty act of vandalism by a gang of youths described in the morning paper. Father was violent in his denunciation of the boys involved.

"Oh, I can understand them," I averred. "Boys can do crazy things. I was a vandal myself once."

"Really? What did you do?"

As I told them about the Thorndike playhouse, the room became strangely silent. Father was actually livid.

"You did that," he almost whispered.

He then told me that the chief of the Bar Harbor police had called on him and taken him to view the devastation. "I'm sorry, Mr. Auchincloss, but we have to investigate every child on the hill."

"You think a child of mine could have done *that*?"

"And the chief actually apologized!" Father almost shouted at me now. "And he didn't even interview you!"

"You can't be mad at me now!" I protested.

"I'm not so sure," he retorted. "That police chief is probably long dead by now. I can never apologize to him."

7

Bar Harbor

MY FATHER USED to say of Mount Desert Island, which is just off the Maine coast and contains the once very fashionable summer resort of Bar Harbor, that it was so beautifully unreal that one could hardly read the New York newspapers there, with all their threats of doom. This made it, of course, an ideal vacation spot, and we used to rent for midsummer a commodious stone and wood villa on a peninsula called Schooner Head that had the sea on both sides. Our landlord, who laid fishnets along the rocky coast around the peninsula, hauled in a blue shark one morning and laid it out on the small beach at which our housemaids sometimes dared to take an icy dip. There was no other place for them to do that, but needless to say, after the sight of the shark none of them ever put even a toe in the water again.

Of course, we as a family had the elegant swimming club where the water was let in at first from the ocean to a large enclosure and warmed before being piped up to the members' pool. We had also a golf club and marinas for those who sailed or enjoyed deep-sea fishing. The sumptuous shingle villas along the seashore blended handsomely with the gray of the rocks and the deep green of the surrounding hills, which we called mountains. It was indeed a paradise for the rich.

Both my parents were old Bar Harborites—my paternal grandparents still in my boyhood occupied their big house on Clefstone Road—but it was the natural beauty of the place rather than its social activity that attracted them to it. Father, who was something of a jock, adored the golf and tennis, and Mother's particular joy was in climbing the mountains and planning picnics. Of course, they had plenty of old friends on the island, and dined out on occasion, but they always insisted that that was not the "point" of the summer, which was essentially a family occasion. They avoided the spectacular new rich like the plague, and even the old if they were too involved in the social game.

This meant that we children were not invited to children's parties given by parents on whom ours had not chosen to call, and these, of course, tended to be the most lavish and desirable of all. My older brother and sister didn't care, but I resented it bitterly. I tried to make out just what Mother's standards were and listened carefully when she talked to her friends without knowing, so to speak, that she was on the air. Here is the explanation that one of her intimates gave to her question as to how she could bring herself to dine with a particularly vulgar tycoon:

"But I love it, my dear. You start with strong, well-mixed cocktails followed by a cordon bleu dinner at which you needn't talk to the ape on either side of you as you are expected to listen to a fine organ expertly played. And after dinner there's a brand-new and exciting movie in a comfortable auditorium. Oh, I can't wait to be asked again!"

But that was not at all Mother's idea of a good time. She deplored the deep impression made on me, her third child, by the very people she sought to avoid. There were, however, people on the island at whose great houses she had to go because of family connections. One of these belonged to Mrs. Duer Blake, the former Mrs. Clarence Mackey, who gave large parties for the children of her second marriage (including my friend Billy Blake), where the winners of games received little cups of real silver that I craved but never won. I thought Mrs. Blake, tall, thin, and aristocratic-looking, the epitome of style, and it further fascinated me that one of her eyes was of glass. We were always told not to stare at her in the effort to find out which one.

One day Mother had come to pick me up after a Blake party. As she was taking leave of our hostess, I was startled to hear Mrs. Blake say of the next meeting of this children's group (which was scheduled to be at my grandmother's house): "I'll send the children, of course, but you know I can't go there."

"Why can't Mrs. Blake go to Grandmother's?" I wanted to know as we drove home.

"Because your grandmother is very old-fashioned," Mother replied in a rather tart tone. "She won't receive women who've been divorced and remarried."

I was appalled. Dowdy old Grandmother wouldn't receive

glamorous Mrs. Blake! I had evidently a great deal to learn about society, which was a tangle of rules that made no logical sense.

I was much helped in my quest by my friends Edith and Jimmy Clark, with whom I sometimes stayed for a week after my family had returned to New York. Their parents had each been married four times, and they lived for long stretches with their maternal grandmother, Edith Fabbri, the divorced Vanderbilt wife of Ernesto Fabbri. He was one of three Fabbri brothers whose father had been an Italian partner in Morgan & Co. The other two were bachelors: Egisto, a man of fabulous good taste who designed for his sister-in-law Buonriposo, the Palladian villa in Bar Harbor where I stayed, and Alessandro, famed radio expert and inventor who became Edith's lover and is buried beside her in the Vanderbilt cemetery in Staten Island. Visitors assume the tomb is her husband's. The Fabbris were rich, but Edith was richer and considered the essence of respectability on Mount Desert Island, though everyone knew everything about her. I was learning.

Her past did not keep Mrs. Fabbri from disapproving of most of her grandchildren's friends, whose parents she considered of too recent origin to be invited to Buonriposo, but this did not keep Jimmy and Edith from going. Bar Harbor, like many social summer resorts, offered the new rich a chance to break into a society that barred them at home. Let us suppose, for example, that you have made a fortune from some unattractive aspect of plumbing in Philadelphia and are not received by the better families. Invest your money in Mount

Desert Island, where your yacht, your glittering, foreign cars, your fabulous parties will be the envy of the younger generation, who have not yet developed their parents' snobbishness. The latter will not object to their young going to your parties, for they do not imagine a summer friendship commits anyone to much. But they may find, on returning to Philadelphia, that their children will have formed deeper friendships than they have expected—even love affairs—and it will be hard to ignore their parents.

I learned in Bar Harbor that sex is as interesting to people I once regarded as too old for it as it is to the young. The mother of my friends, Teresa, was the most beautiful woman on the island, and on her rare visits to her mother when she was between marriages, and sometimes not, the telephone at Buonriposo rang constantly for her. There was an extension in my bedroom, and I had the impudence to listen in. Was that really Father's friend Tom Cook, whose amorous tone I heard? It was. Yet he was married to a friend of Mother's and had six children, some of whom were older than I. Even so.

The young were less social snobs than the old, but they had equally rigid standards where personalities were involved. They could be hard as nails on an unattractive girl, which my late friend Mariska de Hedry, for all her sterling qualities, unhappily was in youth. She was the only child of a former Hungarian diplomat, married to an American heiress who crossed the Atlantic every summer to visit her sister, Miss Coleman, in her big house on the Shore Path. The family was hopelessly conservative and old-fashioned, and Mariska's dismal plainness was not alleviated by her dowdy if expensive clothes. The jeunesse dorée of Bar Harbor wouldn't give the poor girl the time of day, but I appreciated her character and saw her from time to time. One day she asked me to take her to the Saturday night dance at the swimming club, which she ordinarily never went to, adding, as if to explain: "The emperor is staying with us, and Mummie thinks he would like the dance."

It was a command performance from her father's former boss, the Austro-Hungarian emperor pretender Otto, and of course we three went. Word of whom we had brought spread like fire around the dance floor, and Mariska found herself the belle of the ball. For fifteen minutes. By then the beauties of the summer colony had entirely preempted the imperial pretender, who was only too willing to be preempted, and I was left with Mariska, who soon enough told me that she was ready to go home and leave Otto to his new friends.

Bar Harbor was not the place for her. It was not the place for saints, one of whom, as a nun, she almost became.

◇◇◇ 8 ◇◇◇

Bad Sports

I MUST BE CAREFUL in writing about my first two years at Groton School, the famous boy's (in my day) private preparatory academy. During my days the institution existed under the administration of an Episcopalian priest (Endicott Peabody) and was located in Groton, Massachusetts.

My first two years here were a time for me of great unhappiness. I'm aware that it is all too common for persons dilating on their childhood woes to blame them on schools, teachers, parents, anything and anyone but themselves. I assure you that this is not my tendency. While it is true that I was badly trained academically at Bovee for Groton, I had brought a lot of things on myself that were incompatible with a happy boarding school life.

I had contributed to my athletic incompetence by avoiding sports at Bovee whenever I could. I had also increased my unpopularity there by confining my social life to the least ambitious jokesters who could offer little in terms of social experience for my upcoming years. Why I had not prepared I cannot say. At Bovee, all the while, I had ominously suspected that at

Groton I would be no longer protected by family and friendly teachers, but rather at the mercy of a majority of the sort of cruel boys whom I had been mostly protected from. And so indeed it turned out just this way. I had a sorry time before I learned to cope.

I had just turned twelve when I was sent to Groton and up to that time I had, except for my premonitions about the place, been a moderately happy child. On the night before leaving my parents, my brother John (already a sixth former at the school) and I attended a performance of *Sweet Adeline*, because John was a fan of Helen Morgan. I well recall the sickening feeling in my stomach as she sang, "'Twas not so long ago, that Pa was Mommie's beau." I knew that my old life was over.

The beauty of the Groton School campus, with its circle of fine red-brick buildings and handsome gray Gothic chapel, meant nothing to me, despite the genial welcome of the pleasant masters. I knew that I was, suddenly, on my own and that all the nice things that had hitherto protected me—Bovee, dancing school, even the Greys and my parents—themselves were no longer available.

The trouble started right away. Carrying my fresh new textbooks to the schoolhouse in the morning I approached a large boy who I had learned was my second cousin, Gordon Auchincloss. Without suspicion, I introduced myself.

"Why hello, Cousin!" he cried in what I naïvely supposed was a friendly greeting. Then he gave me a rough shove that drove me backwards upside down over his pal, who was kneeling behind me. My new books lay scattered in the mud. Welcome to the real Groton, not the Groton of a benign faculty or a benevolent board of trustees!

Much worse was to follow. Early on I departed for Groton Village, as was allowed on Saturday afternoons, for an ice cream soda, with two other boys. Passing over a bridge we foolishly cast a few stones at a train passing underneath. Unfortunately, one broke a window in the engine room, and an angry complaint was made to the headmaster. He then asked a class I attended if we knew anything about the assault. I thought it incumbent on me to make a full confession, as I so often, since my days of thievery had ended, was wont to do, whatever my own level of guilt in the matter. I did so, unfortunately and carelessly involving the two other boys. It was an attempt at honesty and, as so often occurs with such forays, disaster was the result. At Bovee we had never heard of the crime of "snitching." I thought I was being virtuous. Well, that did it.

A non-Buckley boy in a class heavily stacked with Buckley alums, I became even more of a social leper. I could expect to be struck or kicked as I passed from classroom to classroom or even to be beaten up by a mob. I had no friends and was even subject to a sexual violation that would have created a major scandal today. Yet I must emphasize that every person in the administration of that school would have been horrified had they known what was going on. They were helpless then just as their counterparts are these days. Boys cannot be shielded from one another. Nor did I ever complain, either to a parent or teacher. I believe it was all part of the inevitable process of becoming a man in a dreary world.

I was perfectly aware that many boys played games in the cubicles at night called "mutual masturbation." I doubt if these included sodomy; the very word might have frightened them off. This practice left little aftereffect that I could see: not one member of the form became an acknowledged homosexual in maturity. But there was one difference separating this sort of relationship between boys in England and America. In America it was never called love, even by the boys themselves. This would have been regarded as hopelessly degrading to their masculinity. In English literature you find terms suggesting homosexuality used quite freely about youths who would later happily forsake their own sex to become the warriors of the light brigade. What we call the bad habits of naughty boys can develop into the military force that sustains an empire.

Certainly one of the most mysterious and memorable figures to emerge from my youth was Jimmy Regan, longtime senior master at Groton School. He was the executive officer, to use a naval term, to the all-dominating figure of the Reverend Endicott Peabody, founder and veteran headmaster, whose exact opposite in character and personality Regan appeared to be. For he was a wispy little man, impossible to associate with the mildest athleticism, perfectly dressed, of quiet good manners yet curiously forceful, who took for granted that he had succeeded in establishing his absolute rule on the campus and need no longer raise his voice. He deferred only to the head-master but there his deference was complete.

Regan was precisely what a great headmaster needed, and Peabody was well aware of this. The spirit, the fire, the leadership of the school was all provided by the principal; it was Regan's job to look into every corner and cranny of the institution and be sure that the machinery was working. And tactfully or even ruthlessly correct it if it wasn't.

Regan was regarded with something like awe by the faculty and boys; they felt his power but one didn't see it. He was always equable, always reasonable. Little was known about his background. Small wonder that there were those who thought he might once have been a Jesuit priest. He would have been a good one.

But he was always a kind and benevolent man, and he eased the burden of administration on the aging shoulders of a greater one to whom he was passionately loyal. They were a great team. And in the summer vacation Jimmy Regan went to a little village in the north of France which had suffered cruel damage in World War I and where he found ample opportunities for charity from what seem to have been his adequate private means.

In my day, the young, unmarried masters who gave so much to the intellectual life of a boys' boarding school were eyed quite closely by the often suspicious and wary members of the administration. A very discreet closet gay, particularly if elderly, might be tolerated on the faculty so long as no boy was ever given a suggestion of the teacher's preferences, but others less careful faced challenges. A popular and attractive master at Groton was let go for having a sentimental summer correspondence with a handsome boy—no touching even alleged.

It was commonly said, at least in his French class of my year, that Mr. Regan, parading past our chairs as he spouted, with a perfect Gallic accent, from our text, would sometimes pause before a particularly robust boy and rub the back of his neck casually and sometimes even slip a sly hand down the back of his trousers, his fingers approaching the backside.

He was playing with fire. How could he dare? Because he never went further. And knew he would never go further. The boy would never complain and knew he would not be listened to if he did. The groping could be explained as unintentional. Still, it was much commented on among the boys. We all love to bring the great down to our level or lower.

Some years ago at the American Academy of Arts and Letters I encountered a fellow member, George Rickey, the world famous sculptor, then ninety, who, as a charming and very muscular young man, had briefly taught at Groton. I asked him to dine, and he replied: "Gladly, but on condition that we discuss nothing but Groton School in 1933."

I agreed, and before our meal was finished we happed upon the old rumors of Jimmy Regan's sexual tastes.

"Of course, even the faculty heard those rumors," he told me. "One day he invited me to go into Boston with him for a concert. We would spend the night at his club there, the Somerset. He drove me in his big Cadillac, and after the concert we went to his room where we undressed and got into our pajamas. He then placed a bottle of gin on the table between our beds. Now, I thought, if he ever tries anything, this will be it. We had a drink and went to sleep. Nothing happened."

Nor do I think anything ever did. Jimmy Regan was a good and conscientious man. He did not believe that pedophilia was proper conduct for a teacher of male youth, and he was never going to give into its urges. Others might have different views; that did not concern him. What he was given to do in this life, he would do perfectly and that was all that need concern him. If he occasionally let himself show a trifle too much affection for a fine-looking youth, it could not possibly do the latter any harm, for even if the boy was not one to reject a same-sex relationship, he certainly would not choose one with a small, wispy old man.

At last, after a dormitory party in which my every extremity was covered with flung ice cream, there was a lull in my persecution. The evening was broken up by the arrival of the kindly dorm master who rescued me and sent the others to bed. Then he helped me look for my dental biteplate, which had been lost in the fray. I told him it had cost my parents $100, an astronomic sum, and for the first time I burst into racking sobs. He was kind to me as nobody had been, found my biteplate, put his arm around my shoulders, and sent me to bed almost consoled. (He was the same man compelled to leave Groton after his letters to the handsome boy, but I always recall him with the deepest affection.)

As I have said, a lull now followed, as it seemed my persecution had begun to bore its leaders. I even picked up one or two friends. Then I had an aggravated case of tonsillitis and had to go home for a couple of months, and finally it was, blessedly, summer. I behaved as I had been, by example, taught. That is, I made no mention of my unhappiness. Not a single complaint about school was directed to my parents during the long hot months, and they had no reason to think that things weren't going well, except that my marks were poor. My father was a graduate of the school himself and under the same headmaster, but he would have taken me out of Groton in a moment had he suspected the truth. He was a rare thing, a jock who never reproached his son for not being one.

My mother suspected that all was not well for me at school and spotted the redness on my tongue in September when it was time to go back to the seat of my torture. I had smeared it with Mercurochrome in an effort to make myself ill so that I could stay home. Not surprisingly, given my mother's perspicacity, it didn't work. But on this occasion, perhaps chastened by the previous year, I didn't dare confess. The redness was attributed to something I ate, and I was duly returned to Groton as a second former.

A new problem awaited me. My Latin teacher, Fritz DeVeau, a dry, sarcastic bachelor of independent means (he spent his summers in Bar Harbor where his wit and acid realism made him popular even with my parents) filled me for some reason with a paralyzing awe. I was not doing well in Latin anyway, but I was hopeless when translating for him. He would give me a daily zero on a recitation, simply commenting: "Another goose egg, Auchincloss." It was said mockingly in the class that my marks looked like a chain across the page. This affected me in other classes, and the faculty actually began to discuss the advisability of my repeating a year. Mother came to discuss it.

The idea of adding a whole year to my Groton sentence of six filled me with a wild terror. I would literally have preferred death. But in my desperation I conceived a plan of escape.

"Get me dropped from 2A Latin to 2B," I begged Mother, "and I think I can make it."

Mother, reluctant as perhaps never before to interfere (perhaps even she was cowed by Groton's hallowed halls) with the school administration, recognized the extent of my misery. She brought herself to tackle the formidable and veteran headmaster, who told her that my teachers believed I was simply lazy.

"But what can we really lose?" she argued, attempting to advance my plan. "He seems morbidly terrified at the idea of repeating a year."

God bless her; it worked. I knew it was a great concession, and I was resolved to make good. Like a drowning man clutching the lifesaver that had been finally tossed to him I fought my way to the shore. I entered the classroom of 2B Latin and was greeted by its master, Mr. Andrews, a stout, dumpy, funny-looking middle-aged man who had been promoted to the faculty from being the headmaster's secretary and whose face bore a huge purple birthmark. But—forgive the cliché—he had a heart of the purest gold.

"I hear you've come down to us because you're lazy," he said. Then he winked at me.

How I loved that man! My marks turned around.

In the following year my grades soared from the bottom of the class to the top, and I was returned to the aegis of the once terrible DeVeau, who now appeared to have been a paper tiger and, indeed, became a friend.

I had finally found a chink in the Groton wall through which I could crawl, if not to any great popularity, at least to the respectability of high marks. I could now afford to eliminate all hated sports from my life except for the minimum required by the school schedule. At home I continued to enjoy a game of tennis, but the only spectator sport I ever indulged in was the bull fight, on a rare visit to Spain or Mexico, and this I soon gave up as too bloody. But the unfortunate effect on my personality was that I allowed myself to consider this turning of my back on athletics as the sign of a superiority of character, and I made something of an ass of myself at Groton by not attending matches with visiting teams and scorning any manifestation of "school spirit."

This led, at one point, to a clash with my roommate, Bill Bundy. He and his younger brother, McGeorge, would later become world famous as security advisers to presidents Kennedy and Johnson and ardent supporters of the Vietnam War. In fact, they earned from David Halberstam the ironical title of "the best and the brightest," despite the fact it was they who helped plunge us into disaster.

Well, returning from the Groton library where I had spent a Saturday afternoon *not* attending a football game with a visiting team, which we had lost, I found Bill actually in tears over the defeat. Foolishly I mocked him, and he was so angry that he arranged to have a new roommate. We made it up later, but it was not the best way for me to make friends.

Although McGeorge was in a lower form, he was the younger brother who became the better friend of mine. Both brothers shared an intense feeling about internecine sport, and I have sometimes wondered if the spirit of "Groton must not lose" did not play a role in their reluctance to face defeat in an unwinnable and unnecessary war.

Mac, as president of the dramatic society, chose for his annual play Shakespeare's *Henry V*, of which he seemed entirely to accept the conventional interpretation that it is a hymn to patriotic and military glory.

But this was only so far as the king is depicted in his heroic speeches. The faculty coach, Malcolm Strachan, who believed that Shakespeare was seeking secretly to convey his own pacifist credo in the lines of the clowns, persuaded Mac that it would make a more interesting production to portray both interpretations. At any rate, what stood out was Mac's splendid acting as Henry V glorifying a totally aggressive war. I cannot help but note that it is recorded that, in difficult moments of the Vietnamese conflict, Mac recited some of the speeches he remembered from *Henry V* to LBJ.

* * *

When I was president of the dramatics club, the year before Mac, I should have had the lead in the play chosen, Molière's *The Would-be Gentleman*. Yet my cousin Gordon Auchincloss—last seen in non-theatrical circumstances—was considered better for the part. This was disappointing, and I had to content myself with the secondary role of Dorante, but much worse was to follow. In my principal scene with the elegant marquise Dorimène, I clumsily sat on the edge of a curtain dropping to the stage. So tight did I pull it that the audience feared it would come down, and so missed all the words.

9

Religion

I CANNOT RECALL that religion played any important role in my life until I went to Groton School at the age of twelve. The Auchinclosses, being of Scottish origin, were naturally Presbyterians, and in my grandfather Auchincloss's generation very strict and sober ones.

My grandmother Auchincloss, of English descent, born a Russell of New York and Newport, belonged to the more fashionable Episcopal church, but as a dutiful spouse, she accompanied her husband on Sundays to his Presbyterian temple. Unlike him, as it happened, she was very devout, though it did the poor lady little good at the end when she died in an agony created by the fear of hell's fire. Her ending confirmed my father in his lifelong antipathy to religion.

"I never knew ease of conscience and independence of mind," he told me once, "until I wrapped up religion once and for all and threw it in the East River."

Yet a more moral and honorable man never drew breath. He taught me that there was no necessary connection between Christian faith and Christian conduct.

* * *

As children we often accompanied Mother to church on Sunday while Father played golf. She was interested in religion, but as a part of philosophy in which she was widely read; it never seemed to answer an emotional need in her. For her offspring the celebration of religion was pretty well confined to the sentimentality of the Christmas story. My older brother, whom I much admired, made no secret of his firm atheism, and when I asked him if he didn't even believe in an afterlife, he assured me that I might survive just long enough to hear his mocking laugh.

At Groton, the massive personality of Endicott Peabody, then in his late seventies and known as the Rector, dominated the campus. He had founded the school half a century before. My father and half the fathers of my classmates had been his students; they were as much in awe of him as we were. There was no appeal, at least in our minds, from his decrees. We came almost to identify him with the deity whom he so passionately and articulately adored. To doubt any article of his creed would seem an impertinence to an absolute authority.

Ultimately I came to recognize that the rector had a benignant side, that his love of the school he had created was genuine, and that his concern reached out to every boy under his jurisdiction. Watching him praying strongly aloud in chapel, one noticed how his eyes sometimes closed, how his great body almost quivered with emotion. It was hard to believe that God did not hear him or carefully consider his positions. A species of minor but sentimental religious ecstasy was born in me at this period.

I decided with the sanction (or was it the indifference?) of my parents to be confirmed into the Episcopal church, because, of course, the rector would do the confirming, and I attended his conferences on the subject where he gave to each boy present his unmistakable personal attention.

Greedy to be singled out by the great man, I would ask questions in the answers to which I had no real interest, such as: Was it sanitary for so many to sip wine from the same communion cup? I simply wanted that large balding head turned in my direction and that intense gray-eyed stare fixed on my puny self as I heard the grave response: "Others have been concerned about that, my boy. You may have noticed that after each communicant has drunk I give the cup a strong wipe with my napkin."

After my confirmation I remained a believer until my graduation from Groton. I had no trouble with the creed. I said my prayers at night, and I rose early to attend Holy Communion on Sundays, which was celebrated before the school breakfast. But one day a friend of mine, a deeply thoughtful Boston boy whom I much admired, Sam Shaw, suggested, as we happened to be walking past the then-empty chapel, that we enter and sit there for a bit. We did so for perhaps a quarter of an hour. When we came out, Sam said, "That was fine, wasn't it?" And it *had* been fine, though I knew that Sam embraced no religion whatsoever. Nor has he ever subsequently. Yet our little visit struck me then and still does as a deeply religious moment.

Later I would return to the family Presbyterianism, but my faith was largely gone, and never really came back, even in some tight moments during the war. I came to share the amiable agnosticism of so many of my contemporaries and endeavored to live up to their moral code. I found the Christian sexual taboos unnecessary.

I played for a time the sophomoric game of picking holes in the gospel, correcting the predictions and doubting the miracles, but ended by rejecting the virgin birth and settling for the theory, tacitly held, I believe, by millions of so-called Christians, that Jesus was simply a gifted mortal. I could never even give the church credit for good lives; it seemed to me that it valued faith above all, and I couldn't see why it was virtuous to believe in a god and sinful not to. I could quite see, however, why it was important for a church that we should.

What I could never quite eliminate from my evaluations of the religions of the world was the death and mayhem that they had inflicted on people who questioned their creeds. It seems that as soon as the banner of a new faith has been firmly planted in converted soil, its priesthood invents savage punishment for heresy.

It's all very well to argue that, at least in the case of the worshippers of Christ, physical retribution has been abolished, but it took force to make the churches agree, and they have retained the concept of hell to let them perpetrate in the hereafter what they can no longer accomplish on earth.

I recall a performance of Verdi's *Don Carlos* at the Metropolitan Opera where the auto-da-fé scene was brilliantly and effectively staged. The condemned heretics marched glumly across the stage toward the explosion of light in the wings representing the fire that awaited them. Mrs. Clare Boothe Luce, famous Catholic convert, in the box next to mine audibly protested. I had the impression that it was the representation of the past rather than its condemnation that really upset her.

How far back in the past was burning still an acceptable form of execution in supposedly civilized countries? I believe a woman was burned alive for the murder of her husband in England in one of the first years of the nineteenth century. And it is possible to put ourselves in the mind of long-dead people who, with perfect complacency, did things of hideous cruelty, if those things happen to be described by a vivid and sympathetic writer.

Take Madame de Sévigné, for example, who wrote such copious letters to her beloved daughter. It is hard not to love a woman so kind, so witty, so seemingly humane and sensible, so like the finest women of our own day. But what is this that we encounter? The marquise is going along with a family plan to enhance her grandson's inheritance and his chance for an advantageous matrimonial match by transferring his sister's dowry to him and locking up for life the poor little robbed thing in a convent!

"Oh, she will be quite comfortable there," the grandmother coolly opines. "The abbess is her aunt." "On est la niece de Madame!"

* * *

Saying all this brings me to the question of what influence Christianity had on my contemporaries at Groton and later. I don't think very much. Few as adults even attended divine services, and only two became priests. We heard, it was true, of a devout group of boys at Saint Paul's School in Concord, New Hampshire, and one who became a Trappist monk, but this was rare. Was the Ivy League of my day then a godless one? Perhaps so, but it certainly did not lack ideals.

I used to say to my father: "If my classmates should ever run this country all would be well." The irony of my life is that they did indeed have a hand in it. And every one of them was a fervent backer of the war in Vietnam.

10

The Great Depression

MY SIX YEARS at Groton, 1930–1935, coincided closely with those of the Great Depression, but the Great Crash of 1929, which devastated our world, affected my family little, though we had reason to regret the move we had just made to a splendid penthouse on the highest point of Park Avenue. I was completely absorbed by boarding school and essentially unaware of the outside world until I had to go home to have my tonsils out. I needed a tutor to make up for lost school time, and Mother asked me if there was anyone from the old Bovee faculty I would like. The school was terminated; the teachers were all out of work.

"Oh, I'd love Mr. Evans, but you'd never get him."

"Oh, I think I might."

And poor, dear Mr. Evans duly appeared, looking sad and gaunt. Mother, leaving for her day, told me to be sure to ask him to stay for lunch. I forgot, and when she returned and found him gone she was irritated.

"Why was it so important?" I wanted to know.

"Because he's hungry!"

* * *

During these difficult times, Father remained a member of the Davis Polk firm, and there was always an income to be gleaned from the financing and reorganization of the great corporations it represented. When things were so bad that the older members had to reduce their percentages of the take, they would do as John Davis instructed them. He would take each older partner aside and say, if to Father, "Howland, we old farts have to move over a bit."

Sometimes, as Father put it, when the figures came out, it would be apparent that only one old fart had moved over, but that was all right. Davis's charm and the eminence of his political and legal career lent weight to his decisions for the firm. In a brilliant but competitive partnership it was always helpful to have a strong leader.

In the early years of the Depression, there came a time when Father was seriously concerned, without validity, about a corporate bond issue that he had approved: Would the firm have to buy it in? Would he survive financially? Then his father, John W. Auchincloss, lost the bulk of his fortune on the stock market, and my father's siblings blamed him unfairly for not guiding the doddering old man with a firmer hand. My poor parents had a nervous crackup, and we didn't know where we were at. Despite my sympathies for the disadvantaged, I sometimes think economic insecurity is most taxing when sudden and when its victims are least accustomed to bearing it.

Mother purported to derive comfort from my fourteen-year-old's smart-alecky sagacity. "It's the end of something," I told her pompously, "but not of everything."

Despite these ruminations the bad luck ended as suddenly as it had come. The bond issue was not invalid, after all; my grandfather's affairs were somehow patched up. Father recovered and went back to work.

I have never understood my grandfather's financial career. His older sister Sarah returned to Scotland and made a fortunate marriage to Sir James Coats, the great thread tycoon. Grandfather, as a young man, formed a partnership with his brother Hugh Dudley called Auchincloss Brothers to represent Coates Thread in America. They did so well that Grandfather was able to build a summer house in Newport that is still one of the show places of that opulent colony. Yet when Sir James asked him and his brother to take into their partnership an American son-in-law of Sir James, they refused, saying they would choose their own American representative. So that golden business was lost. Grandfather went into other enterprises, some of which failed, and lost his directorship in Illinois Central by talking back to E. H. Harriman. He lived well all his long life, but he was losing money even in the bull market of 1929, and when he died in 1937 he left an estate of only $300,000. His brother Hugh Dudley had done better; he had married the daughter of one of John D. Rockefeller's partners. That there was something a bit cloudy in Grandfather's upper story may explain his belief that an ancestor called Stuart gave him a claim to the throne of Scotland.

My father's older and my mother's two younger brothers did well enough for themselves in the Depression and caused no concern in the family, but this was less true of Father's three sisters. Aunt Betty, the eldest, had married Percy Jennings, son of the famous and wealthy corporate lawyer Frederick B. Jennings, whose mansion on lower Park Avenue later became the Princeton Club, but whose wealth was largely dissipated by poor family investments. Fortunately, there were some trusts in a bank to ward off total disaster.

Aunt Caroline, wife of a rich doctor of the Fowler meat-packing family, was the hardest hit, as her husband had invested heavily in mortgaged brownstone residences that were foreclosed on him. She used to say that she sometimes took the Madison Avenue trolley in lieu of the Fifth Avenue bus to save a nickel. Finally there was that perennial victim of hard times, the unwed daughter, my aunt Josie, who became a trained nurse, unique in our family, who used to mildly complain that it was hardly fair to raise a daughter with expectations of economic means and leave her to fend for herself.

At school in the Depression I heard a great deal of families "cutting down," but in our world it was largely the luxuries that were being eliminated. The children even of the hardest hit were apt to be kept in private schools, often on scholarships originally planned for the impoverished classes. Innumerable cousins and friends still managed to get out of the hot, hot city in summer.

I think the dividing line for me between the pre-1929 Depression days and all that followed was the line of huge derivative

French chateaux and Italian palazzos that lines Fifth Avenue from Forty-second Street to Ninety-sixth. Almost all were destroyed by the 1920s and '30s. They had been erected to show off the new wealth of business leaders in the economic boom that followed the Civil War, and many, particularly those commissioned by the Vanderbilt clan, were designed by Richard Morris Hunt, whose sculpted image appropriately adorns a colonnade of the park side of the avenue near Seventieth Street. Some of the mansions were handsome enough, but the prevailing look was vulgar. It is hard to imagine anyone living in them today.

It might be difficult today to find men or women who take themselves that seriously. For how can you live in a palace without occasionally imagining yourself royal? We still have rich, even super rich, but they know they're not royal. The guests so festively attired as kings and queens from Mrs. W. K. Vanderbilt's famous costume ball in the 1880s may have been not so sure.

11

The Brits

I ADMIRED THE WAY Queen Mary occasionally appeared, covered with jewels, in the New York Sunday rotogravure, but I found that my admiration was not shared by my Irish nurse, Maggie. When I asked her once if the queen had to go to the bathroom like ordinary people she retorted: "She does, and makes a big stink."

Yet Britain played little role in my young life though my ancestry was totally English or Scottish and, with the exception of the Auchinclosses who did not leave their native Paisley until 1803, went back to colonial days. Little contact remained between the American and Scottish branches except for one important one, that between my grandfather and his sister Sarah's husband, James Coats, the severance of which led to a grave reversal in my grandfather's hitherto successful business career.

I remember my mother's story of her first emotional contact with British history. It was at a school assembly on a January morning of 1901 when the headmistress, Miss Chapin, announced to the girls that the sixty-four-year reign of Queen

Victoria of England had come to an end. And she added: "I am going to ask Priscilla Stanton to recite for us Lord Tennyson's dedication of the *Idylls of the King* to the memory of the Prince Consort, which I know she has by heart."

Mother, aged thirteen, suddenly inspired with a courage hitherto unknown to her, sprang to her feet and rang out the lines, ending with the invocation to the widowed queen: "Till God has placed thee at his side again."

Miss Chapin murmured reverently: "And now God has placed her at his side again." Mother used to say, not entirely in jest, that, like Pheidippides, she should have died then and there, at the peak of her glory, and that her whole afterlife had been an anticlimax.

We didn't go to England as a family until I was fifteen, and then I was thrilled as never before. To me it was like my history book illustrated. I saw King George leaving Westminster Abbey with the little princesses; I counted the double line of Rolls-Royce limousines, each with a coat of arms painted on its door, parked by the Ritz; I reveled in the grandeur of Windsor, and Blenheim. But there was one unfortunate occurrence. There was a drought on, and the newspapers urged their readers to emulate His Majesty and use only an inch of water in their tub. My room in Flemings Hotel on Half-Moon Street was directly over the reception desk, so that the scandal of the tub that I allowed to overflow while I was distracted with a movie magazine was apparent to all.

Standing with my father in the crowded elevator the next

day I had to listen to the speculations of the outraged hotel guests. "Who caused that shocking flood?" "They say it was a Yankee boy." "Oh, of course. You might have known."

Father gave my ear a painful pinch. "Listen to them! And they're right, too."

The English are too polite to tell us what they often think of us. I had several experiences during the war while my ship, an LST (landing ship, tank), was operating out of ports in the English Channel. On liberty I would take myself sightseeing. Amphibious officers tended to dress carelessly, particularly when not on duty, and it was sometimes difficult to tell just what we were. As I have a bit of an English accent I was often taken for that by drivers who picked me up when I hitchhiked.

"Are they as bad where you are as where we are?" they would sometimes ask. "I suppose I should tell you I'm an American naval officer." "Oh, I beg your pardon."

I understood that it was a hardship for many to have two million GIs parked on them in the south of England. Our boys on the whole were fine, but American arrogance, particularly about their superior equipment, can be hard to take.

Certainly over the years of my adult life the old legend of the arrogant British has dwindled to almost nothing. But it was very real once. The possession of a world empire of "half of creation," as Kipling put it, and the assumed duty of policing "lesser breeds without the law" hardly engendered humility, and even a slight perusal of English nineteenth-century fiction gives one startling examples of just how superior the superior people used to feel. Jane Austen's Lady Catherine de Bourgh strikes us today as a caricature, but was she? A peer's daughter in *Jane Eyre* commands a footman to "Cease your chatter, blockhead, and do my bidding," and the Duke of Omnium, Trollope's model for the perfect British nobleman, finds it difficult to accept for the wife of his heir a beautiful and cultivated American girl whose father has been considered a potential presidential candidate. In my own day I knew an imperial relic in India who paid his help by tossing coins at their feet as they stood before him.

Trollope, whose important position in the post office carried him to all parts of the empire, was certainly one of the great reporters of his day. In his numberless novels he invariably defines the exact social class of every character, supplies his income and the origin of his family, and even lets us know whether he is content with his position in life or hankers to improve it. Class is never neglected. To what is called a gentleman, however, and this is never quite clear, except that it is more a matter of character than of wealth or title, more doors are open. He, as in *The Duke's Children*, may even aspire to Omnium's daughter, though it's going to be a struggle. And Elizabeth Bennet in *Pride and Prejudice* tells Lady Catherine that the fact alone that she is a gentleman's daughter qualifies her to marry the millionaire grandson of an earl.

I would have, some years later, the chance to witness an instance of the disappearing arrogance of aristocratic Britain. I had been taken by a socially well-connected friend to a very swell house party in a great castle in Wales. It was my only such experience and I was much awed. Of course I knew nobody but the friend who had been allowed to bring me, and my hostess, who had a great title and even greater wealth, thinking that anything might be expected of an unknown and probably impecunious Yankee, took upon herself, perhaps as a kindness, for she was as charming as she was blunt, to warn me that her daughters would have only a pittance, that everything went to the heir.

She also referred to an American lady, also staying at the castle as a friend of one of her sons, as "common," which she certainly was, though it would have surprised me to hear an American hostess so refer to a houseguest. But English aristocrats of her day said what they pleased, when they pleased, and to whom they pleased. In a way it was rather attractive.

12

Cohorts

I GRADUATED FROM Groton School in 1935 with twenty-
eight other boys. Their future was not undistinguished. I
became a recognized novelist and president of the American
Academy of Arts and Letters. William McCormick Blair, the
number one aide of Adlai Stevenson, would be our ambassador to the Philippines. John Brooks was president of the Cela-
nese Company; William P. Bundy was an assistant secretary of
state and close adviser to President Johnson. Marshall Green
became ambassador to Indonesia and Australia. James Hig-
gins was president of the Mellon Bank, and Eben Pyne of City
Bank. Stanley Resor was secretary of the army, and Robert
Whitney would have almost surely become president of J. P.
Morgan & Co. had he not been killed in an auto accident. Arthur Gardner also would probably have been heard from in
his very untypical Groton career as a Jesuit priest had he not
succumbed early to polio, released from his vows so that, dying, he could wed the wonderful nurse who attended to him.

Not a bad showing for a small class, but what was even more
remarkable was that all the others, if less spectacular, had suc-

cessful business or professional careers. There was not a failure in the crowd.

Although, as I have stated, my years at Groton coincided with the worst period of the Great Depression, there was no instance of radical or revolutionary political activity on the campus. Alfred Kazin, the great literary critic and my contemporary, told me once that in his West side Manhattan boyhood everyone he knew had been a communist. I replied that in my East side no one I knew had been.

It was a bitterly divided society but the repercussions were not felt at Groton except when our Scottish history teacher, George Rickey, married on a vacation a radical girl from Greenwich Village and brought her to the school. She soon made her contempt for the smug faculty wives and the "stuffy, spoiled little boys" so manifest that her connection with both them and her genius of a husband had to be severed, and he was left free for the splendid artistic career that soon opened before him.

I, however, remained true to the family conservatism. A few years later, when F.D.R.'s presidential campaign motorcade came through New Haven where I was a Yale freshman, I waved a huge sunflower, Alfred Landon's symbol, in front of it and got struck in the face by a policeman. It was not until Jack Kennedy that I voted for a Democratic president.

The families of most of the Groton boys had not only been Republicans but were bitterly anti–New Deal and anti-F.D.R., though the president was a graduate of the school himself and had sent his sons there. We boys were less impassioned than our parents and enjoyed the hustle and bustle and circling of motorcycles that accompanied the presidential visits to the school. They seemed to put us on the map, and I was even proud of a relationship to the great man.

Father used to claim that the fact that the president's father's first wife had been a Howland cousin did not make us blood kin, but he didn't realize that there had been three Roosevelt-Howland marriages and that he and F.D.R. were indubitably third cousins. New York, however, unlike the southern states, pays little attention to cousins more distant than first, and as there were dozens of people in town in the same relationship to the president, many of whom were not proud of it, it was not a matter of note in our family.

Overall, I was not especially concerned with things political. At Yale I continued acting with the dramatic society there until I appeared in a Goldoni comedy as a girl disguised as a boy, and my father did not think that this exhibition of confused sexual identity would enhance my image in the college. No doubt I took his criticism too seriously. Father and his Yale classmates were rather what we called too bulldog, but in my disgust I gave up the dramatic society altogether.

I continued to be stagestruck and went to New York frequently just to go to the theatre. I remember with a particular thrill John Gielgud in *Hamlet* and Nazimova in *Ghosts* and *The Cherry Orchard*. Indeed Nazimova's Mrs. Alving was a unique dramatic experience for me; I went three times to hear her tell her true life story to the incredulous pastor, and I was fascinated at a later time to read Tennessee Williams had given Nazimova in this role as a factor in his becoming a playwright. I like to think that we may have attended the same performance.

Later in life, I would write several plays, but such was never my thing. The only one that was ever produced was a one-act piece called *The Club Bedroom* with a cast of three women. A production required only a set with one portrait (an empty frame would do for an imaginative audience). It was done on Channel 13 and several times off-Broadway. I attended every performance, and later, when my wife, Adele, asked me why, I replied with a quip from the *New Yorker:* "Infatuation with the sound of one's own words department."

The theatre is indeed a dangerous Lorelei combing her golden hair with a golden comb over the vessels wrecked on the rocky shore below her, and it took a real effort for me to give her up. The trouble is that one always sees one's unproduced drama as it is splendidly enacted in one's imagination. The rejected novelist sees only a manuscript and a bad one.

The would-be playwright may also be misled by associates in the trade. The theatre world is a world to itself; to some in it nothing else is real. I remember a cocktail party given by Worthington Miner, the producer who was then planning to do a play of mine about which he later changed his mind. The guests were all theatre people, except one, Mrs. Miner's uncle, whom nobody recognized but me. In any other gathering he would have been the center of attention as James Byrne, governor, ambassador, secretary of state, and U.S Supreme Court justice. But here he was nobody.

As I have said, perhaps too often, given my firm hold on the notion, that at no time in my youth was I an athlete. Far from it, I confess. Nor did I have any interest in or admiration for such greats. My father was an excellent tennis player and once scored a hole-in-one on the Piping Rock Club golf course, but in accordance with the extreme generosity of his nature, he never dropped even a hint that he was disappointed that I hadn't inherited any of his facility or interest in this area.

Very different were the men of my mother's family, the Stantons, whom I favored in appearance, and who shared some of my athletic disability without any of my compensating indifference to it. My brother John, for example, slaved over his tennis, and later golf, as if his very life depended on them, without achieving more than a decent competence, and Bill Stanton, who had moved to Hong Kong where he could afford to devote his life to horses and polo, became only adequately adept in the latter game, despite numerous nasty falls.

I'm afraid that I viewed these two men's obsession, as I saw it, on the subject of sport with a faint contempt, as if they were worshipping a lesser god than mine of literature. It has often struck me that, at least in their case, there seemed to be a relationship between the care they took over their personal appearance and the pains with which they trained themselves for their favorite sport. I was on a motor trip with Uncle Bill in Europe when he suddenly realized he didn't have the right suit for the club in Singapore to which he was bound and he cabled his "number one boy" in Hong Kong to put one on the plane for him. I could have almost lived on what my brother expended on shirts and cufflinks. Neither man was possessed of the least ambition for getting ahead in the world, but they both cared strongly about how they looked and how people with whom they associated looked, and whether the latter's manners were good and how they behaved, and what sports they played.

13

A Hang-up

I N MY YOUNGER years I was subject to a severe emotional hang-up that had a purely negative effect on my personality. The problem was not immediately apparent to friends or family. Not surprising, as the concern was a strong tendency to reject indignantly any sexual approach to myself made by either girl or boy. It was as if I were actually defending myself from a blow.

With boys this was confined to an occasional nightly visit to my cubicle at boarding school where my angry refusal was quickly accepted, for those caught were liable to expulsion, and who wanted an unwilling partner, anyway? Later on, in college, such invitations ceased, because those so inclined had learned to recognize each other or make discreet inquiries. Only a very handsome male was propositioned without some checking, and I was not that.

The girls of my age and world were on the whole much less bold than today and did not expect to be pawed on an early date, or even a later one, with the result that I had many close friends of both sexes and remained, until cured by a brilliant psychiatrist, an unsuspected virgin. For I never mentioned my problem to a soul until I sought medical help. I was too deeply ashamed of it.

I knew, of course, that something was wrong. I was acutely aware that it was not normal to dislike occasions in locker rooms where men were stripped and eyed each other. Of course, there were no such occasions where we were exposed to nude women. Except one. My mother loved picnics, and on a fine summer day in Maine when my family, parents, brothers, and sister were enjoying one by a lonely lake, Mother suggested that we all take a dip. "But we didn't bring our bathing suits," I pointed out.

"Oh, that doesn't matter," she replied. "There's just us here. Let's be natural and not artificial."

The others agreed and started to strip. When it was seen that I was not complying I was urged not to be stuffy, and my older brother genially took a tug at my shirt. And then I flipped and gave way to a fit of wild hate. I don't even remember what happened but the family recognized with shock and dismay that they had better let me alone.

Well, what was it? It was obvious that I was defending something with my life. The brilliant psychiatrist decided that something had happened to me at age two, something of course of which I was now totally unaware. He wanted to talk to my mother, and she, always open-minded, agreed. She then told him something that had much worried her. I, at two, had shared a bedroom with my sister who was just under four. Because she masturbated, as most children do, and there were still doctors at that time who deemed this bad for a child's health, let alone the child's morals, Mother consulted a famous relative, a noted and noble-minded surgeon who was not, however, versed in psychiatry.

He prescribed that my poor sister be swathed in a thick species of diaper so that she could not touch her private parts. Mother was dubious about this, but the putting on and the taking off of this blanket led to my sensing when it came off that my sister was missing something that I had. Would it be my turn next? Here, according to the psychiatrist, was the source of my feelings and caution.

This fear of castration could now be treated and gradually eliminated, and I was duly returned to normalcy. But it took a while. How many lives have been ruined by people's identification of sex with sin! Or by other people's attitudes about what constitutes proper love or sex. My friend Jack Woods comes to mind.

In Clare Boothe Luce's play *The Women*, the pretty manicurist who is engaged in stealing the heroine's husband shows little sympathy for the woman she is robbing because the latter, anyway, has "all the important things." By this she presumably means the family and the social position, things of far greater value to the poor manicurist than the stupid male who has fallen for her charm.

The people who have social position are inclined, at least articulately, to downgrade it and consider as simply vulgar those who too obviously seek it. Oscar Wilde put it well when he said "to be in society is simply a bore. To be out of it is simply a tragedy." But one can still sympathize with those who feel the lack of an assured position in society. The secure person can enter a room of strangers with the confidence that he is just as good as any of them, no matter what title they may devise to describe themselves, and be simply amused by any who deem themselves superior to him. If they exceed him in rank, legally, militarily, or however, that is because the political system calls for ranks and not because one person is entitled to look down on another. In any orderly society, rank has its function.

I sometimes think that the desire for what one doesn't have is what makes the world go round. I think the greatness of Theodore Dreiser's understanding of the human psyche is demonstrated in his ability to make his reader not only comprehend but actually feel the passionate craving that another human being may have for things about which the reader may have nothing but indifference or even scorn. Sister Carrie's attraction to the cheap baubles in the window of a variety store become as real to us as Clyde Griffith's yearning to join the tacky society that occupies the lakeside summer cottages of his small town. It is the not having, the not belonging that becomes all. Ernest Hemingway is supposed to have said of John O'Hara that when he died, he'd go to Yale.

Jack Woods, with whom I roomed for two years at Yale, would have understood that. He was neither handsome nor athletic, and he had neither money nor social position. He was the only child of an obscure New Jersey businessman, a suicide, and his dreary Catholic widow. But he had little doubt that his brilliant mind would bring him what he wanted, and it did. When he needed money he would check cash prizes in competitions, enter them, and win. He got high grades without seeming to care for cards.

But what he desired was to mingle with the socially elite and be a guest at the most glittering New York debutante parties. He was a devout epicurean; he told me once that the one thing in life he could not bear was to hear that someone was having a better time than he was.

That he used me unsparingly in his successful social club showed his cleverness. The leaders of the class were not at first available to him, but I was, and I knew them all. And it was easy for me in New York to take him as my houseguest to almost any debutante party. Why did I allow myself to be so used? Because Jack never made any secret of what he was up to, and his company was invariably delightful. He always, so to speak, paid his way, and I think he was as fond of me as he was of anyone, which was not much.

Besides, he read the stories I had begun to work on—we were both on the Yale *Lit*—and I believed him the most acute of critics. When he said of one tale of mine, "For the first time you've been boring," I was overjoyed, for it implied that at other times I had not been.

Did he have any morals? In sex I don't know; that was a subject he didn't often discuss. But he certainly showed a bad side when he entered into a successful plot with his father's mistress to cover up the evidence of the paternal suicide so that they might collect and share the small life insurance policy. When I reproached him with this and told him it was a crime, he burst into tears and said it was all very well for me to talk that way with a rich father, etc., etc.

"It's still a crime," I insisted.

He blubbered but kept the money.

Jack's attempts at fiction, which appeared in Yale *Lit*, showed a good deal of wit and were decidedly clever, perhaps a bit too self-consciously so. He might well have become an established writer; he was too smart to have failed to correct his errors. What he really lacked was a warm heart; he might have become a Ronald Firbank or a lesser Evelyn Waugh. But on graduation he chose what may have been the field of his greatest aptitude: reporting. I saw less of him now for I was at law school in Virginia. He went to work for the *New York Herald Tribune*, where his pieces soon attracted the notice of its great owner, Mrs. Ogden Reid herself. She had decided to send him abroad as a war reporter when he suddenly ended it all by committing suicide.

Why? He had been staying with me at my parents' apartment, and we had both been ushers at a classmate's wedding on the afternoon of the day he did it. We had separated after the reception, and he had gone to several parties, ending up in the apartment of Stewart Alsop, brother of Joe. Jack was sitting on a window seat by a wide-open window (it was a hot June night), rocking himself precariously back and forth until he fell suddenly out the window to his death.

He had been drinking heavily and seemed in high, even

wild, spirits. It could have been an accident, had it not been for the letter that he left for me at the family's apartment explaining that he fully intended to end his life that night because of the agony of finding himself simultaneously in love with a man and a woman.

I knew both the persons involved; they were attractive and excellent individuals, good friends of Jack's, but quite unaware of the passion he concealed. He liked to have dates with society girls, but they were never serious, and he showed no sign of being gay. If his emotional situation was as he described it, it is probable that his feeling for the man was greater, for marriage to the girl (always a possibility) would have been regarded generally as an excellent thing for him, and in 1941 homosexuality was still in the closet. It had to be strong to grip the feelings of a man who desired public respect.

Kill oneself over a sexual infatuation? With a future like Jack's? Well, people do. The great Ms. Reid summoned me to explain it to her, and I couldn't. Jack was forever an example of how well one can know a person without knowing him at all. The horror of World War II might have broken up his self-obsession and sharpened the genius of his powers of observation. But wars are better at killing people than changing them.

In my early years I don't recall homosexuality, or any sexual irregularity for that matter, being discussed by the "grownups" in the family or their friends. No doubt it was to keep a distasteful subject from children's ears, but I imagine that there were a good many closets to which the subject had been relegated. People generally knew what was meant when a woman was described as "horsey" or a man as "effeminate." But it was certainly true that an enormous social stigma was attached to any open demonstration of "undue" affection for a member of one's own sex, and a reputation in that respect meant an automatic exclusion from any men's social group. Women were considerably more tolerant and more changeable: lesbians often ceased to be lesbians. On the other hand, if the "vice" were successfully closeted—and this was not difficult—society was not inclined to pry. As in so many things appearance was everything. Indeed, in the sweller circles prying was considered actually bad manners.

At Yale, homosexuality was tolerated but discountenanced. It would almost surely have disqualified a man for a senior society or even a fraternity, but he was not condemned. I remember when I was befriended by the son of a world famous automaker, and my father simply mentioned to me that he had a police record for solicitation, that I dropped his acquaintance like the proverbial hotcake. There were enough hurdles in life without that one.

During the war I had a sordid experience with the dreadful captain of the LST in the Atlantic of whom I shall have more to say. Everyone in the navy knows that when a vessel has been enough months at sea without access to women that some curious things go on in the crew. A sensible officer doesn't see anything. But my crazy captain was shocked, despite a life in the navy, and forced me to make a ridiculous investigation.

More than half the crew had been engaged in what most people would call homosexual activity, but if you told them that they would react with violent indignation and insist their manhood had been insulted. They hated gays!

Certainly, in those early years when I apprehended a mysterious physical hurt from any sexual urges cast in my direction I must have included romantic love as a door far better left unopened. Indeed, I came to regard love stories as tragedies. But I was never such a fool as to think my views shared. I was quite aware that most people were highly enthusiastic about love, and the more intense it was the more desirable. Great passions, even when they brought destruction in their path, were deemed the most desirable of all, at least to readers or theatregoers. Somehow or other great passion became associated to me with great character, and the leading male of a romance was apt to seem to me a hero. By great character, I should immediately add, I do not mean goodness. It was not at all necessary that he should be good.

Joseph Wood Krutch, a deep admirer of the dramas of Eugene O'Neill, wrote "that human beings are great and terrible creatures when they are in the grip of great passions." But is this really true of the Mannons in O'Neill's greatest and most terrible drama, *Mourning Becomes Electra*? Christine Mannon poisons her husband so clumsily that her daughter catches her, and her son Orin simply goes to pieces after killing her lover. Are these spectacles really at once "horrible and cleansing"?

It seems to me that Racine is closer to what came to be my concept of tragedy than even Shakespeare. He was deeply bathed in Jansenist religiosity, similar to our Puritanism, and repellent though this may be to many of us, it avoids all sentimentality on the subject of sin. Sin is never in Racine "magnificent." It is a loathsome, disfiguring, and humiliating disease that is nonetheless shameful for being inflicted on the sufferer by a capricious god for no fault of his own.

14

I Begin to Write

I HAD WRITTEN short stories for the school magazine when I was at Groton and had begun to take a serious interest in reading the great English novelists of the nineteenth century. This was much encouraged by a wise teacher of English at Groton, Louis Zahner, who had the wisdom to teach the boys the actual pleasure of literature. I needed this badly because I was inclined to regard both the reading and writing of fiction as primarily a way of balancing my failure to achieve anything like what schoolboys regard as real success. This was justified to my immature way of thinking when my grade of 100 percent in the English college board entrance examination was celebrated by the school by declaring a holiday. I imagined I was really getting somewhere.

A French course that I took under Professor Joseph Seronde in my sophomore year at Yale changed my life. He taught nineteenth-century French fiction and drama, and I found myself electrified (there is no better word) by *Madame Bovary* and *Le Rouge et Le Noir*. But it was by no means only by such famous classics that I was thrilled. I was no less excited by such lesser works as Daudet's *Fromont Jeune et Risler Ainé*, by Hervieu's *Peints par Eux-mêmes*, and by Dumas fils's *Les Idées de Madame Aubray*. Indeed, there was not a single novel or play assigned in the course that did not bring me absolute delight, and delight was something that I had not previously expected from literature. I knew now that the novel form was going to play a significant role in my life, though just how I had only a dim idea.

In the meanwhile, why not write one? I had plenty of time at Yale; preparation for the courses was not hard, and even if I kept an evening free for the movie with friends (Joan Crawford, Norma Shearer, and Clark Gable seemed to dominate our lives), the afternoons were utterly unoccupied. The Linonia and Brothers Reading Room of the Sterling Library offered comfortable alcoves where one was never interrupted, and I started work on a novel that was partially inspired by *Madame Bovary*.

My heroine, whom I called Audrey Emerson, was to be endowed with half of every human quality; she would be half ambitious, half erotic, half intellectual, half honest, half unscrupulous, and so forth. By never being a total anything, she would wreak havoc in the lives of others. She would be born the discontented member of a lower-middle-class family that had once been upper. Her particular prey would be an idle, impecunious, but popular extra man in the highest New York society called Beverly Stregelinus, a name supposedly suggestive of a certain silliness in his nature. Beverly was a bit of an ass, but I tried to endow him with a soul.

The book came swiftly; a few months completed it. I felt an intensity of happiness in writing it that may have been equaled in later days but was never exceeded. I am aware that joy has not always been associated with the creative process, and the reading public often likes to think of its authors as suffering as they compose. Indeed some may, but I still suspect that Shakespeare went to a bar and had several jovial drinks after leaving King Lear in the storm and Desdemona with Othello's pillow on her face. I had my manuscript typed and sent it to Scribner's.

My novel was rejected but with an appreciative letter urging me to send them my next book. At twenty I should have been delighted. But no, I was grabbed by the folly of youth and decided in a fit of depression that I must give up all idea of ever becoming a writer and immediately drown myself in the study of law in any creditable law school that would accept me now, on the basis of three years at college. The University of Virginia Law School was one such, and I applied and was accepted. My poor father who paid for everything uncomplainingly urged me to at least finish at Yale. But, backed by Mother, I insisted and the following fall found me duly enrolled in Virginia Law, from which I graduated in 1941.

I took a private oath that I would write no more, certainly never while law school was in session, and the latter part I kept, but in the two summers of my law school years I wrote another novel that I destroyed. I threw it in the garbage pail and later, too late, tried to retrieve it. As I remember it, it was no loss to letters. I did not write again until the last year of the war when my ship was undergoing extensive repairs in port, and then I wrote the novel that was ultimately published as *The Indifferent Children.*

It is now time to describe the role that my skeptical mother, Priscilla, played in my writing career. She had thoroughly approved of my leaving Yale for law school. A woman with a firm sense of the necessity of one's filling one's proper role, she had always been obsessed with the notion that hers—assigned, I believe, by incomprehensible gods—was the maternal one, though it was the role for which she was least qualified. Instead of leaving her children blessedly alone she interfered reluctantly and unsuccessfully in their lives.

She took an early and unfortunate interest in my writing. She decided not only that I had no outstanding talent but that my efforts showed a worldly streak that if published would make me look vulgar and hurt me with serious people in any career that I adopted. She believed that the world needed second- and even third-rate lawyers, doctors, dentists, etc., but that it had no need of artists and writers except the very best, of whom I would certainly not be one. She had no doubt that I would do perfectly well in a nonartistic career, and she sincerely, even passionately, believed that she was sparing me misery in aborting any literary choice on my part.

She was so upset by the decision of Prentice-Hall to publish *The Indifferent Children* that she brought all her heat on me to use a pen name, and I weakly succumbed. She was con-

vinced it would hurt me in the eyes of the partners of Sullivan & Cromwell. But, of course they didn't give a damn. Yet
Mother was never convinced that I might make a go of writing as a career, even after I had brought out several books that
sold quite well and were favorably reviewed. When I married
she was afraid my wife's family would disapprove of the novel I
published at the time. They didn't.

When she came around at last to my side it was much later
with the appearance of the one novel I would have thought she
would have most feared. In *The Embezzler*, published in 1966,
many years after I was established as a novelist, I described in
exact detail the crime of Richard Whitney, once head of the
New York Stock Exchange and brother of the senior partner
of J. P. Morgan & Co. I even read the text of his trial to get it
right.

But the characters in the novel were not even remotely
based on members of the Whitney Family. Nonetheless, Mrs.
George Whitney, wife of the head of Morgan, and herself the
daughter of a Morgan partner, a formidable social presence in
New York and a friend of Mother's, got wind of what I was doing and asked me to kill the book, as yet unprinted. I told her
that her brother-in-law's crime was an integral part of American financial history and available to all. She said yes, but
people had stopped talking about it and that my book would
be a bestseller and start them up again. This turned out to be
true, but I could hardly give in and didn't.

Why wasn't *The Embezzler* Mother's nightmare? Both her
family and Father's were tightly linked to the House of Mor-

gan. She used to say that she was relieved of her concerns by Martha Whitney whom she apparently fancied looking over her shoulder when she read anything of mine. When Mrs. Whitney requested that my novel not be published, Mother snorted: "Who does Martha think she is that she can demand the suppression of Louis' book?" And she came down solidly on my side where she remained for the rest of her life, reading everything I wrote in manuscript and giving me wonderful advice.

At Yale, as far as preparing myself to write, there had been nothing for me to aim at. I had no interest in the *Daily News* or any fraternity or senior society. It was not until law school that the concept of competition entered my life. Admission to Yale had been easy and in those days cost my parents little. Like most of my friends I took the whole college business for granted. None of us really went to work until professional school or a first job. Then we did.

15

Sea Duty

DURING ALMOST ALL of 1941 we were still at peace, although it was beginning to seem inevitable that we should enter the war. England, which had seemed fated to go under in 1940, had survived thanks to the heroism of the Royal Air Force, and most of my friends were either applying for military commissions or actually in training for them.

Much earlier I had applied for a commission as an ensign in naval intelligence on the theory (not yet wholly discounted) that we might never get into the war and that this would be the most comfortable way to avoid the draft. It was, however, widely regarded as a way of seeking a noncombat position, and I'm afraid this was a factor in my thinking. Mother was active in "America First" antiwar activity—anything to spare her sons the risk of gunfire—and I had tried to persuade myself that the best way to end the European conflict was by a stalemate. It would also be the safest and easiest solution for myself.

As the war clouds darkened the skies at home, I began to feel ashamed. A weekend spent with Bill Scranton in Scranton, Pennsylvania, convinced me that shame, indeed, was what I should be feeling. Bill's mother, a remarkable woman and a great Republican leader in her state, made no secret, although never offensively, of her poor opinion of men who in any way sought to avoid combat in the coming conflict.

Mrs. Scranton to me was a kind of saint. All the servants in her large household were ex-convicts for whom, when she deemed them ready to return to society, she used her considerable political power to get jobs fitting their skills. But her old butler refused to go, telling her, "When I leave your service, Ma'am, it will be feet first."

Returning home I put in an application to the navy to change the commission sought from IVS (Intelligence Volunteer Special) to DVG (Deck Volunteer General), which meant that I should be sent for sea training, with so many of my friends, to the old battleship *Prairie State*, moored up the Hudson. Its graduates were ensigns known as "ninety-day wonders," and I slept easier at night now that I thought I had removed a blot on my character.

But the imps of comedy, who are always on the watch, were not going to let me get away with anything as easily as that. Sea duty I should have, a couple of oceans of it, but I should pay first with a year of misery. Pearl Harbor struck, and with it came the unwelcome intelligence commission and orders to proceed to the Panama Canal Zone. To protest that I was waiting for a different commission would look like avoiding an overseas assignment and was impossible.

* * *

Before actually leaving for the Canal Zone I was briefly on duty at 50 Church Street interviewing persons who had endorsed applicants for intelligence commissions. Were such endorsements based on a true knowledge of the candidate or were they simply family or business favors? Often the endorsers were men or women of public importance whom we interviewers were anxious to meet, and there was a good deal of swapping of names behind the scenes.

I remember an eager young lawyer swapping the lyric soprano Geraldine Farrar for two justices of the Appellate Division. It was all mildly diverting, and I still hoped for a reprieve to the *Prairie State*, but no. Orders to the Canal Zone duly arrived and I found myself for wretched months in a tropical office, a bureaucratic nightmare, where my job was to check Americans passing through the zone to South America against lists of semisuspects, including people who had Japanese servants! And all the while my friends were transiting the third lock of the great canal nearest our office on their way to battle and sometimes to their death. Oh, the imps of comedy knew their job.

Even when they finally relaxed and let me go to sea, it was for some months a touch ludicrous, for it was aboard a former luxury yacht, essentially useless to the war effort. The navy didn't know what to do with us, so we were sent, in the interest of the Good Neighbor policy, to Guayaquil to train Ecuadorian midshipmen. While there, for some unknown reason, the cruiser *Concord* steamed in on her way to a Far East destiny, and we fell under her jurisdiction. As senior officer afloat,

I was assigned the duty, with shore patrol of four sailors, of cleaning out the Guayaquil cathouses at midnight. Of course they were full of the *Concord's* crew. I would be entertained by the madame with a rotten native brandy while my men roused the sailors upstairs. It was easy work, for in wartime naval discipline really operated, and when it was over I and my foursome posed for a fine photograph, which I sent to my mother without explaining what it was.

Father had an aunt, Jane, widow of his mother's brother, Charles H. Russell. He had been somebody special to us as a founder of Stetson, Jennings, and Russell (later Davis Polk), Father's firm. Aunt Jane, a tremendous war hawk, was a great character and someone on whom it was incumbent for me to call when I came home on leave. All visitors had to view respectfully a huge cardboard hoisted on an easel in her living room, on which were pasted articles and photographs relating to the heroic deeds of her relatives and friends in the war. My photograph, taken in these somewhat compromising circumstances, soon appeared on Aunt Jane's easel. This led the imps, who knew the tale behind the photo, to laugh their fill, but by this time, my application for amphibious duty successful, I had more pressing concerns for I had been given a glimpse of reality on the Normandy beaches.

16

Fear

AT SOME, NOW HARD to place moment, I found myself in the Atlantic Ocean, part of a crew of 103, absurdly large for a vessel that was nothing but a sea truck that traveled in convoys protected by destroyers. The British LST, identical with ours, both having been made in the United States, was run with equal efficiency by a crew of twenty.

The navy didn't choose its best personnel for amphibious vessels, and we had onboard boys from the hills of Tennessee who had inherited prejudices originating in the Revolution and who hesitated to place foot on English soil even for liberty. We had four black sailors who under the navy's Jim Crow policy had to be officers' stewards, but they loved England where, as one of them told me, they were treated like human beings.

The oddest man I had onboard, appropriately called Valentine, informed me when we were actually under way for Normandy that his battle station had been changed to a 20 MM gun. "And I'm a conscientious objector!" was his outraged complaint. And indeed he was; some naval clerk had mixed up his papers. But he was a reasonable man and finally agreed he would not be helping the war effort if stationed in the laundry.

The officers, except for the captain and engineer who were mustangs, temporarily commissioned chief petty officers from the regular navy, were all young college graduates and pleasantly helpful to me. One of the difficulties college men had in the war was adjusting themselves to taking orders from men of obviously inferior intelligence. This difficulty did not affect any of my friends who had been to boarding school. The one thing that had been thoroughly taught there was that orders and reason have no necessary connection.

One of the most difficult things a man can suffer is fear. It is worse for a man than a woman, for in addition to the pain involved he is often disgraced, as a true man is supposed either to be above fear or able to keep it hidden. Courage is universally admired, and much decorated by the military, though it may be a free gift of the gods to the rare souls who are born with the luck to be fearless.

An army psychiatrist in World War II stationed on a Pacific atoll told me of rushing to a plane that had just made a crash landing and seeing the pilot emerge unhurt from the flames. His pulse was normal! Was he a freak or a hero? Theodore Roosevelt maintained that any man can conquer fear by training his imagination, and this seems to have been true of him and his sons, who defied fear in war and in big-game hunting, but I cannot believe that it is possible for all men.

I am not speaking of fear of misfortune, which is simple apprehension, but the dread of deadly harm to oneself. Some-times the harm is imaginary like that of ghosts or large insects or reptiles, which can inspire unreasonable panic. But more often it is real. In World War II, I served as a naval officer and found myself in some tight spots, particularly in the English Channel where my LST operated as a kind of military ferry between the English ports and the Normandy coast. What I most feared about fear, particularly on times when we loaded in London and had to pass the Straits of Dover only eighteen miles from the bombarding German guns, was that I might black out and be unable to perform my functions. This never happened, but on one occasion I had the unpleasant experi-ence of hearing myself say something that I was completely unconscious of having articulated. It was a simple case of hysteria.

We were anchored off the coast of Normandy waiting for the tide to go down to the point where we could beach the hefty vessel (it was 330 feet long) and unload its tanks and am-munition trucks. We were pretty much at the mercy of low-flying German planes, and one struck us with three bombs. Two went through two bulkheads and disposed of themselves harmlessly in the water. A third buried itself in the back of a truck on the tank deck filled with ammunition. It did not deto-nate, but if it did, it was the end of our ship.

Where was the captain? Locked in his cabin where he was probably drinking. He was a mustang, a regular navy chief petty officer, raised only for wartime to the rank of commis-sioned officer. Many of these made splendid officers; he was an unhappy exception, an alcoholic and a coward. I now found myself practically in command.

But what to do? I went down to the tank deck to examine the lethal object sticking out of the truck. Did one pull it out? Neither I nor any of the ship's officers or crew had any instruction in demolition.

And then a calm English voice (we were carrying British troops) breathed in my ear. "I know it's your bomb, sir, but if it goes, it's all of us. I have a demolition squad onboard. Would you let me handle it?"

Never was a request more eagerly granted. Following the helpful British officer's instructions I ordered the opening of the bow doors and got him a stretcher from sick bay and watched while his men withdrew the bomb from the truck, handling it as if it were a baby, and placed it in the water.

After that I took him to the wardroom and got him a drink of forbidden whiskey. It was then that I heard my own voice distinctly utter words that certainly did not come from my conscious self.

"There's another of them."

"Jesus! Where is it? Let's go."

"April fool."

"Not very funny."

I was too mortified to apologize, and anyway what I had said was unforgivable. Of course it was hysteria.

I felt the greatest admiration for the heroes we were now bringing back from a front that was moving rapidly into Germany.

Once we took onboard the survivors of a ravaged company of paratroopers. They were drinking coffee in the wardroom, which they had mildly messed up when the captain came in wearing a silk Chinese robe and called them pigs. He left the room before they could kill him, which they easily might have, for they were formidable warriors and had no idea who he was. When I explained to their irate commanding officer who reported the incident to me the identity of the man who had insulted them, he would only be satisfied by my public apology on behalf of the navy. You can imagine what this did to my relations with the captain. But I didn't care. I knew he would not dare to complain to our superiors.

There were no repercussions to the captain's rudeness to these brave men whose valor had been vital to the liberation of France from the Nazi boot, but there had been to his yellow streak, just prior to the Normandy invasion.

Our LST was traveling in convoy on a calm moonlit night on the channel when a British destroyer escort moved alongside of us so close that I, as officer of the deck on the bridge, could hear the British captain through his megaphone. Our captain, as usual, was asleep in his cabin.

"Stop your engines" was the message from our escort. "Survivors ahead in the water." Indeed I could see dozens of heads bobbing on the surface. Obviously what was meant was that we should slow down just enough to glide through them and not cut them to pieces with our big screws. I gave the order, and the captain, awakened by the ship's shudder and rushing to the bridge, wanted to know what the hell was going on. I told him, and he shrieked, "We're under attack! All engines ahead full!"

"Captain!" I protested. "It's only for a minute! And the E-boats are gone already."

"Get off the bridge!"

We plowed through those poor fellows. God only knows what damage we did. Was there a recourse? Against a captain defending his ship? Dream on.

◇◇◇ 17 ◇◇◇

A Return to Society

HAVING WITNESSED WARFARE, I returned to a more familiar battleground where young men were sent for obvious reasons and with mixed results.

The girls whom I knew at home were mostly in their late teens or early twenties and generally belonged to the same society as my family. Most were in college and planning on a domestic career based on marriage. A brief period before the wedding as a secretary or junior magazine editor was sometimes contemplated, and there were always a few adventuresome souls who opted for law or medicine, but these were a decided minority, and the parents rarely approved.

Another minority, of a very different group, chose to skip college and dedicate themselves to the business of being a debutante. Among these were often found the prettiest and richest girls, and the receivers of the greatest publicity, but they also suffered from the taint of superficiality in the eyes of their more serious-minded contemporaries. One prominent debutante confessed to me that she had soon tired of what she called a season of late parties and buying hats, and taken a job at *Vogue*.

For the majority who went to college and elected courses on the sole ground of enjoyment without regard to utility in a future job it was not at all a bad life. Courses in history of art were particularly popular. With the exercise of good judgment and the advice of loving and watchful parents it was not hard to pick an attractive and reliable husband from the circle in which they were raised, and many did. Divorce was the exception rather than the rule in that privileged world. Its privileges were not as commonly wasted as the unprivileged like to think.

In the years before World War I, New York society contented itself for an evening's entertainment with the mansions of its richer members, some of which were equipped with gilded ballrooms. But even the largest of these was limited in size; Mrs. William Astor's notoriously held only four hundred, and the population growth and prosperity of the city soon required more space for the would-be hostess. The great chateaux were now being leveled on the death of their builders; few enjoyed the propriety of more than one owner, and the rich took advantage of the new and easier to run apartment, which could be ordered in almost any size.

Hotels were quick to offer their bigger ballrooms for the now colossal debutante parties, or dinners honoring distinguished citizens or celebrating important birthdays, and charities were quick to perceive how much more could be made by tying an event to a cure for cancer or the building of a new hospital wing. The conscience of the new pleasure seekers was now eased even while they danced and drank.

To become a society leader the aspiring wife of a rich new-comer in the financial world could do little better than join the board of a large and known charity (a vast contribution will sometimes do the trick—if not, double it) and volunteer to help in preparing a charity ball. Don't kid yourself; it can be real work, and the other board ladies will have a sharp eye out for cheats. But they appreciate a good job, and it will pay off. Be sure on the night of the ball to have a knockout dress.

It is fashionable for the attendees of charitable balls to downgrade them, to complain of the interminable cocktail hour, the pushing crowd, the tediousness of the speeches if there were any. Yet look for these critics at the next one you go to, and very likely you will find them. For if they love big par-ties and have the money, where else can they go? It is also true that people hate to feel they have spent their money for noth-ing, and they have bought their expensive tickets from friends whom they expect to hit for their own charities. Yet it still re-mains curious to me how patiently the so-called sophisticated citizens of our sophisticated city submit to hours of ennui just to see and be seen.

A surprising revival in the post–World War II years has been that of the men's clubs; the Colony and the Cosmopoli-tan were saved by their women, but the men had not done the same for theirs. The legend persisted that these institutions were full of ancient gentlemen who dozed in armchairs before ground-floor windows from which they could spy the comely ankles of women passing in the street below. Even the threat of federal legislation requiring them to accept woman members if any portion of their income derived from sales or services to

the public failed to arouse them, and bankruptcy loomed before not a few. Yet suddenly it all turned around. Young men,
it seemed, wanted clubs, and new managements began to offer the pleasures of livelier entertainment: lectures, dances,
concerts, debates, movies, private theatricals. Perhaps most effective of all was the gesture made to women by clubs that
had avoided the law forbidding sexual discrimination. They
granted the widows of deceased members the privileges of
their late husbands. To have a club was now not only to have a
place to go to; it was to have something to do.

In an era where women had become almost as serious as men
about their own professional careers was it possible for society
to produce great social leaders like Grace Vanderbilt, Alva Belmont, and Mamie Fish? From what I have read of memoirs of
the sometimes-called Golden Age of society in the 1890s and
early 1900s, I should think it was very easy. I cannot see that
the hostesses of that earlier era needed much but the habit of
lavish spending. Mrs. Belmont said she knew of no life more
taxing than that of a society leader, but I suspect that her ex-
haustion came from attending more parties than she had to.
She certainly didn't work on making her own entertainments
amusing or intellectually stimulating, nor did the other two I
have mentioned. Mrs. Winthrop Chanler said of the so-called
four hundred, whom she well knew, that they would have
fled in a body from "a poet, a painter, a musician or a clever
Frenchman." She and her closer friends formed a bore insurance society, which paid you a nice little sum of money if you

dined out in New York society and found yourself seated by a listed bore.

The would-be society leader had to spend a fortune on haute couture, but this was spared the men who wore white tie and tails at parties where ladies were present or at the opera, and for bachelor affairs, a tuxedo and black tie. In time the tuxedo became the appropriate uniform for all occasions.

The leading lady of New York society at the end of the twentieth century was certainly Mrs. Vincent Astor, the former Brooke Russell, though she was married to Astor for only six years before his death. This, however, had not been altogether a social misfortune, as he was, however intelligent, a bit of a brute who had hated her friends and wanted to keep her all to himself. She was a woman of infinite charm, delightful wit, and warm affections who had been previously twice married, once briefly and unhappily at age sixteen to the wealthy but unpleasant Dryden Kuser, and then to Charles H. Marshall, the "love of her life," whose widow she became after twenty happy years.

Marshall's sister had married Marshall Field III, and his first wife had been the sister of the first Mrs. Vincent Astor, so Brooke, when she became the third and last of Vincent's wives, took on a "position" with whose duties and privileges she was well acquainted. When she inherited her new husband's wealth she decided to give the bulk of it away. She had the advantage of not being afraid of money and cheerfully willing to part with it. "I know Jayne Wrightsman could buy and sell me several times over," she told me once, "but I still live better than she does."

It was not all that easy, however. It was all very well for the evening social page to call her a queen, but that does not create loyal subjects. There were important people in society who had been permanently alienated by a marriage so crassly motivated by money, for who could marry Vincent for love? "I had to make some new friends," Brooke told me. A ladies discussion group, the Junior Fortnightly, found her not intellectual enough for membership. And the Thursday Evening Club, created to enable the social world of New York to meet professors of its great universities, welcomed Brooke as a member but rejected her nomination as president. Adlai Stevenson, when elected, asked me only half in jest, "Am I now in the true heart of New York society?" Brooke was much admired, but few in society can escape the query, on the least show of superiority, of Who do they think they are, anyway? I admired Brooke for defying this attitude and dressing her grandest and donning her finest jewels when she visited poor neighborhoods to open one of her foundation's works. "They want to see Mrs. Astor," she explained, "and I'm not going to disappoint them."

$\diamond\!\!\diamond\!\!\diamond$ 18 $\diamond\!\!\diamond\!\!\diamond$

The Firm

I N 1941 I WENT TO work in the famous Wall Street
law firm of Sullivan & Cromwell. At that time Sullivan, like
most of the major firms, consisted of some twenty partners and
perhaps sixty associates, so it was possible for all the latter to
know personally with whom they were competing. This is no
longer possible in the mammoth firms of today, and there is
a consequent diminution of anything like the esprit de corps
that used sometimes to exist.

When I was a clerk, the other young men of that position,
almost all of whom were non–New Yorkers and too poor in
1940 and too hard worked to be in a position to enjoy a social life where they could enlarge their acquaintance, tended
to meet together on Saturday night drinking parties. Hard up
though they were, most were married. Success, which came
to a majority of them, altered things considerably, but I am
talking of an earlier year. They were inclined, though always
friendly, to make harmless fun of my background as passé and
irrelevant to modern times, but I would counter by pointing
out that every one of them was "working his tail off" to create

for his children as close a copy of my background as he was able. It was true, and they all succeeded!

The firm was dominated by the Dulles brothers, John Foster and Allen. The former was the managing partner, a great lawyer and future secretary of state under Eisenhower. Allen was less a lawyer than a kind of diplomat; he had many important European clients whose tangled foreign affairs he brilliantly unraveled, making skillful use of the legal expertise of the firm that was always at his disposal. Between them they covered a good portion of the firm's practice. At different times I worked for both men.

Their personalities were almost opposites. Foster was sober, grave, dedicated to work, deeply religious, and utterly unimaginative in his dealing with clerks and staff. Allen, on the other hand, was hearty, cheerful, outgoing, full of charm and humor. Where he was devoted, perhaps too much so, to the fair sex, Foster was strictly a faithful monogamist.

I offer a single instance of Foster's incapacity to deal sympathetically with his employees. I was assigned to the partner in charge of trusts and estates, one who was popular with the associates and used by them as a bridge to the administration of the firm, and I happened to be with him in his office when three of our young lawyers came to consult him. They wanted to know if their fiancées (all were properly engaged) were included in Mrs. Foster Dulles's New Year's Day reception for the attorneys of the firm and their wives.

"Why, of course they are, my dear fellows," my boss assured them. "And very welcome, too."

But one of them seemed to need a further guarantee. "Would you mind asking Mr. Dulles, sir?"

"All right, all right, if you insist," my boss impatiently retorted. He picked up his phone and got the senior partner on the wire. "Oh, Foster, three of our bright young men want to know if they can bring their fiancées to Janet's New Year's party. I've told them of course they may, but they want to be sure it's all right with you."

My boss's face darkened in the silence that ensued. When he hung up he turned away from his visitors. "I'm sorry, my friends, but Mr. Dulles says a fiancée is not a wife."

I doubt if John Foster had any idea that he had just made three enemies for life. A fiancée *wasn't* a wife, was she? Allen, of course, would have shouted a welcome and insisted on being asked to the wedding. Yet, for all Foster's ineptitude and Allen's graciousness, it was the former who had the warmer heart. In the movie about the American spy plane that was shot down over Russia, the actor playing the part of Allen as head of the C.I.A. replies to the officer reassuring him that the captured pilot has a poison pill: "The trouble is they never take them!"

At Sullivan & Cromwell it was thought that this was an unfair picture of Allen's heartlessness. It wasn't.

We were retained by the Bank Worms in France, a vast conglomerate of businesses, to protest the allegation made by a

Harvard professor in a book called *Our Vichy Gamble* that the bank had collaborated with the Germans during the occupation, and Allen Dulles had assigned me to the case. He had very wisely made the point with Professor Langer, the author, that a Harvard professor would naturally acknowledge the truth, if we could convince him of it, and that we would not then have to go to court. It would be my job to do the convincing.

At first this seemed not difficult, as M. Worms was Jewish and had already been cleared in France by three courts of what they called *épuration*. But when you start digging into the dark and muddy field of who did what and with whom during years of business as usual under an oppressive occupying army, you find yourself in a bewildering maze of contradictions. German submarines were constructed in Worms dockyards. Yes, but they never sailed. And so it went, on and on.

I finally assembled a brief that induced a very reluctant professor to take back his allegation. He stated flatly that he would never write another book about a living man. The subject would be too liable to sue.

When I called on M. Worms in Paris, and was about to take a seat before his desk, he almost shouted at me: "Do you care to sit before the arch traitor of Europe?"

"But M. Worms," I protested, "we're on your side. We never believed the Harvard professor."

"Harvard!" He spat the word out. "Well you can be sure of one thing. No descendant of mine will ever darken the doors of Harvard."

"That's all right by me," I assured him. "I'm a Yale man."
He didn't get it.

At a later date, when I had drafted a will for Foster Dulles that
he wished to execute right away, as he was taking a trip, I asked
if I could use his highly efficient secretary, Miss Snell, in the
interests of speed.

"Miss Snell?" he demanded in astonishment. "But Miss
Snell is dead!"

"I'm sorry, sir. I didn't know."

"Yes, she died of a sudden cancer. Perhaps mercifully rapid.
But she had one perfect day before the end. I was still a sena-
tor, and she had lunch with me in the Senate dining room and
afterward she had her picture taken with me on the steps of
the Capitol. Yes, she had one perfect day."

If you can make yourself realize that this came from the
bottom of a heart that really cared for Miss Snell you will have
come a long way to understanding Foster Dulles.

Allen Dulles was the most interesting of the partners to
work for, but it was not for the quality of the legal problem presented but because the value of his great international repute
somehow colored his utterances, particularly his telephone
calls that had nothing to do with the matter in hand. One was
always aware that this was the man who had negotiated the sur-
render of the German armies in north Italy. Of course it was
also the man who had gambled disastrously in the Bay of Pigs.
I always liked what President Kennedy is supposed to have told
him after that: "In England, I'd go. Here, you go."

Arthur Dean, who succeeded Foster as head of the firm, was brilliant when he knew the law and almost more so when he didn't. I remember his explaining to a client what the marital deduction was when it had just been passed and he hadn't even read it. The statute that he made up as he went along (he loved to play games with himself) was a better one than Congress had passed. Of course he was well aware that the clerk attending the conference would get it all straight when it came to drafting the document. God help him if he didn't. I recall another instance when he sat with me in a meeting with a lawyer representing a family attacking the probate of one of our client's wills. He was new to the case, which had already spawned a large file spread out on the table before us and with which I, of course, was familiar. Our opposing lawyer was wantonly rude and offensive, and Dean, angered, started shuffling at seeming random through the papers on the table. In a few minutes he had put his finger on the weak point in our opponent's case that had taken me hours to dig out.

Eustace Seligman brought to the firm not only his genius for diagnosing the essence of a legal problem, but many of his relatives of the great German Jewish financial families known as "our crowd." I recall with particular interest his cousin-in-law, Sam Lewisohn, whose art collection adorns today the walls of so many museums. It was not so much his rather routine legal matters that fascinated me but the personality of this collector. Lewisohn was not the type who bought the advice of an art expert; his pictures were the most important things in his life, and he would sit staring at one, literally for hours, as if taking it in through his pores, before adding it to the sacred collection. He was an early riser, and when I had papers for him to sign I would make a point of arriving at his house even earlier than our appointment so that I would have a moment to slip into the darkened dining room and pull the light switch.

After a brief flicker, the chamber would be gloriously illuminated by Gauguin's *Ia Orana Maria* and Renoir's *In the Meadow.*

Before I left the practice of law I prepared many wills for rich testators, and I encountered the common fear that their progeny would be the victims of fortune hunters. They had hazy ideas of what a fortune hunter was, but they were apt to think of him, in the case of males, as a smooth greasy man of sinister good looks and a phony title. They rarely recognized him as the blue-eyed, blond-haired, athletic, all-American boy next door. They were not often aware, either, that most marriages the world over have been arranged, and many of them happily so. Or that there is very little one can do to protect one's loved ones from their own infatuations.

That a marriage purely mercenary on one side is not apt to be happy in this country I grant, though I can think of some striking exceptions. But where money is only a part of the attraction, guaranteeing the continuance, as a bride or groom may see it, of the comfortable existence both families have accustomed the affianced couple to, it may be harmless enough. Yet many heiresses are haunted by the fear of being married for their money, a fate which befalls many who never know it. For we are all packets of motives and never aware of the sum total of the reasons for our doing anything. Proust gives the example of a woman who marries a man for the privilege of being able to refer to his fashionable aunt by a popular abbreviation of her title: ma tante de Ch'nouville. Is that worse than being married for one's beauty?

A perfect example of a very happy and totally successful marriage that depended heavily on the wife's fortune was that of Wilmarth "Lefty" Lewis and his wife, my father's cousin Annie Burr Auchincloss. He was a luminary of the Yale board and founder of the Lewis Library there, which published the definitive edition of the enormous Horace Walpole correspondence, a monument in letters. This was all done at the expense of Annie Burr, who inherited from her mother a sizeable chunk of the Jennings standard oil fortune. Lefty's whole life was dedicated to Walpole and would have been impossible without the money that Annie Burr lovingly and happily poured into his project. They worked together in everything and brought the eighteenth century to life for innumerable students and readers in their beautiful house in Farmington, now part of the university.

I learned in my many talks with Lefty that he was subject to a curious obsession that some might have called a superstition. He believed, even passionately, that he was being assisted in his constant and worldwide search for Walpoliana (not simply letters but books, furnishings, anything that had belonged to

Horace) by the spirit of the great letter writer himself. Once in the large library of a fellow collector he was told by his dinner host that the room contained a volume once owned by Walpole. He was challenged to put his finger on it and given twenty minutes. He accepted the challenge, and the company withdrew leaving him alone among the vast shelves of books. At first he dashed about seeking to assess the huge library, but at last he decided to let his secret guide do the trick for him, and he relaxed. Just as his time was up and the crowd reappeared he walked calmly to an alcove and placed his finger on the very volume.

Once I dared to ask him if his "gift" had ever operated in a non-Walpole matter. "Only once," he replied. "I was driving from Farmington to New Haven to reproach a curator of rare books in the Sterling Library for failing to bid high enough for an item at auction that I had wanted for Yale. It suddenly came over me that my mission was futile for the man I wanted to see was lying on the floor in the library stacks with blood on his face. I stopped my car and turned it around to go home. Then I thought it was absurd to act on an inner vision, so I drove to New Haven. At the library I was told that my man had indeed fallen from a ladder while reaching for a highly placed book and received a bad nosebleed. But he was all right. I have no idea why the vision was vouchsafed to me."

It was certainly a curious story.

A case revealing a rarely seen side of collecting was demonstrated to me by Mrs. Robert Woods Bliss, the proprietress of

Dumbarton Oaks in Washington, D.C. The collection, if that word is applicable, consists of a splendid red-brick mansion with wonderful furniture of every period, vast and glorious gardens, a small museum of pre-Columbian art, and a huge library devoted to the history of the Byzantine empire, a college for which is located on the premises. I call it a collection because every item in it, including the very pebbles in the garden stream, were imported under the scrutiny of Mrs. Bliss. She was a realist and faced the fact that the world was full of ugliness. Her own fortune had its origin in a vulgar patent medicine for children. All the more reason, she believed, for keeping the nonbeautiful outside the gates of Dumbarton Oaks.

The daily emphasis on beauty is favorable to a certain formality, sometimes suggestive of the past, and this was true of Mr. and Mrs. Bliss, who were in their eighties when they came into my life. She spoke of her own part as if she had been a princess, saying once, "That was the time when they were thinking of marrying me to young Mr. Rockefeller." And she ran a kind of court at Dumbarton Oaks. How she was to address and be addressed by the staff was given careful consideration. Ellis Russell, the elderly bachelor who handled her business, was "Mr. Russell" and she "Mrs. Bliss."

I, as a lawyer, would have normally been treated the same way, but as my elder brother who lived in Washington was on a first-name basis at Dumbarton Oaks, I became "Louis," though she remained "Mrs. Bliss." Jack Thacher, her chief curator and close partner in the whole enterprise, she wished to call simply "Thacher," but he objected and wished to be called "Jack," to which she only agreed if he would call her "Mildred."

After the death of both Blisses, Dumbarton Oaks, their sole residuary legatee (house, gardens, college, and collections) was administered by Harvard. It was generally believed that this was mandated by their wills and could never be altered, but a senior partner of mine, who had a firm conviction that one should never over-empower the dead hand, had at the last moment persuaded the very reluctant Blisses to give their legatee the power to dispose of the entire property by sale. The Byzantine students were now clamorous in their demand that this power be used to move their institute to Cambridge and be run by Harvard proper. They yearned to be associated with other fellow students in a real academic atmosphere. Of course, they had few friends in political Washington who cared for such learned papers as "Plumbing in Constantinople in the Fourth Century A.D."

Rumors began to circulate that Harvard was actually contemplating the use of the power as desired by the students. Would Dumbarton Oaks find itself on the auction block?

I had always been inclined to the liberal side in disputes over how widely to interpret the powers of the charitable fiduciaries faced with difficulty in adapting their mission to modern needs, but I was not indifferent to their moral obligation to deceased founders, and if ever such an obligation existed it was that of Harvard to the Blisses. For decades, they had contributed large percentages of their income to Harvard to support Dumbarton Oaks, always with the assurance that their estates would be wholly devoted to the same end, and indeed on their deaths that promise had been richly fulfilled. It would be shocking indeed to betray them now that they could do nothing to alter the disposition of their funds. I decided that if Harvard so acted it would be incumbent on me to start a letter campaign to the graduates alerting them to what was planned. I was not myself a graduate, but it would be easy to find plenty of people to undertake the job. One had only to recall the bitter fight over the Arnold Arboretum to know how powerful the Harvard conscience could be when aroused. But first, of course, I had to talk to President Bok and Henry Rosovsky, his famous dean of faculty, whose role in the university administration has been compared to that of Richelieu under Louis XIII. I went up to Cambridge and was received by both men. When I had stated my message, the dean asked: "And just what is it that you want of Harvard?"

"Simply your assurance—no binding commitment—that the present status of Dumbarton Oaks will not be altered for a reasonable time."

"And how long is that?"

"I leave it to the conscience of Harvard. With perfect trust."

The dean and the president put their heads together for a brief conference that I could not hear. Then Bok spoke.

"You have it."

It was all I needed.

19

Fleeing the Law

A T SULLIVAN & CROMWELL, the associates were dominated day and night by ambition for partnership. Sometimes they regretted for years a failure to achieve it, even when, as was often the case, for the firm looked after its own, they had moved on to better paying and even more distinguished jobs.

The associates, often married and living on meager salaries, were not apt to be native New Yorkers, and as their rough work schedule gave them little time for social life, their Saturday night drinking parties often included each other or classmates from other law schools. It was in attending such parties that I came to realize a basic difference between us. Whereas in the heart of every man (S&C had then only two women clerks, neither of whom would even be considered for partnership) burned the glow of his yearning to become a member of the firm, in mine was the fear that I might be made one. For the apprehension that I might have chosen the wrong career had already begun to haunt me.

* * *

How had this bizarre situation come about? The novel that I had written aboard my LST in the last year of the war had been published and attracted some favorable critical notice. Nor did it seem to have done me the harm in my office that Mother had anticipated. It was simply regarded as a curiosity, like a fondness for yoga. It was even said that when, at a bar association dinner where John Foster Dulles was jokingly accused of running a sweatshop at 48 Wall Street, he had retorted: "On the contrary. I'm told the clerks all write novels."

Anyhow, the idea had now entered my head that I was destined for a literary career and was perhaps wasting my life at S&C. Might I not in some fashion combine the law with literature?

It was my close friendship with John Raben, an associate in the firm slightly my senior, that persuaded me that the law was ideally too stern a mistress to admit of any partner. He was a splendidly handsome young man, sturdy, well made, with a broad clear brow and a penetrating, evaluating stare, who came of a very different background from mine, the product of urban public schools and the brother of a policeman. He had a brilliant analytical mind and an almost superhuman devotion to and capacity for hard work that ultimately carried him to the headship of the firm in a career interrupted by a fatal cancer in his fifties.

John had a characteristic that might have killed him earlier had it not settled in one line. He hated to stop anything he was doing, whether it was running or playing tennis or making an argument or even drinking at a party. Fortunately for him the activity that won out was work at the office, and he was married to the only woman in town who was willing to give up almost all social life because of her husband's long night hours dedicated to putting the final statement on registration statements. Connie was always willing to stay home with the children.

Was John ambitious? Is that why I put him in this chapter? He was glad enough ultimately to run S&C for he loved S&C and the work it engendered, but it was hard to tell if he had any particular aim in mind. When he started to earn big money, he and Connie didn't seem to know what to do with it. He bought her a mink coat, which she never wore, and when he hired a maid to help her with the housework she asked him what she and the maid would talk about. When they moved to a swell Park Avenue apartment the living room mantel was adorned with the same old family clock that hadn't kept time for a generation. Yet both were happy. And yes, I suppose you could say they had got ahead further than most. He was the perfect corporate lawyer.

John and I were very close so long as I was in S&C. As he was always there our intimacy inevitably diminished when I left. He was a year or two my senior and definitely took the leadership in our relationship, where he could be very dictatorial. I recall a young lawyer in whose future he took an interest but who showed an undue interest in remaining in the Paris office longer than assigned, drawing this *South Pacific* comment from John: "I'm going to wash that Proust right out of his hair!"

* * *

Why he took such an interest in me I don't know, but he seemed to want to train me to be his partner and once actually got me, very much against my will, transferred from my comparatively easy department of wills and estates to the corporate section under his exacting supervision. How I hated it in the weeks before I was unsprung! Night after night with no social life.

But what I saw in John was a total dedication that I then believed was essential to any real accomplishment, be it law or literature. If I was to be a novelist of any worth I should have to abandon Sullivan & Cromwell, and give to writing what he gave to his registration statements. I finally told him this, and he gravely agreed. Neither of us realized that a novelist may be working even when he dreams.

On the rare nights when John was not working he would come to my office and take me to a local bar for a drink that would turn out to be more than one. I shall never forget the night when he was still an associate that I sensed a change in his demeanor. I cannot describe exactly what it was, but something exuded from him. Was it a smile? He was never a great smiler. Was it the way he put his glass down on the table?

"They've made you a partner."

"It's still a secret" was all he said.

I didn't immediately share the news and, not so long after, when I told my father I had resigned from my firm he replied, "I have made discreet inquiries and been told you're doing all right. A partnership is never guaranteed, of course, but you're in the running still. Now you want to quit one of the greatest law firms in the country to write? Who's going to support you, may I ask?"

"You are," I told him, and he did.

But I made one more stab at another profession. I went up to Yale to consult the friendly Bob French, master of Jonathan Edwards College, about the possibility of getting a Ph.D. and teaching English. He told me just how it could be done, and then added: "You've spent years qualifying yourself for one distinguished profession only to abandon it. Are you qualifying yourself for another to treat it the same way?"

I took the hint: if you're going to write, write. And so I did for two and a half years, when I returned permanently to the law. I became a partner in a much smaller firm where I enjoyed a limited but happy practice. But "getting ahead" for me had essentially been shifted to the literary field. I had finally worked out a compromise. That term, in my younger days, was most often used when considering the lives of the other sex.

❖❖ 20 ❖❖

A Few More Words About Women

WHAT IN MY YOUTH was "getting ahead" for women? In my Yale years (1936–1938) it had become quite acceptable, even in the most stylish social set, for a girl to go to college if she so chose. She was not criticized if she didn't want to; to devote one's nineteenth year to the elaborate business of "coming out" was still perfectly acceptable, and the ultimate goal of marriage was still the destiny of any girl, whether a college graduate or not. And of course one could always go to college *and* come out.

At one time a young woman who had reached the age of eighteen was presented to New York society in some form of entertainment, whether it was a reception, a dinner party, or a dance. The invitees were family and friends; there was no particular emphasis on young men. It was not a husband hunt.

The debutante, as she now could be called, was "out"— out of the nursery or convent or whatever guarded enclave her family had used for female minors. Now she could mingle in an adult community as what our Gallic cousins called a *jeune fille à marier*, subject, of course, to whatever were the local rules of chaperonage. After dancing had become the more popular aspect of these gatherings it was inevitable that young men should have become of greater and greater importance until even a modest tea dance, the resort of less-endowed parents, required an orchestra.

As the parties grew in size and came to include other debutantes of the season and their innumerable boyfriends, the family aspect diminished, and the older generation was expected to fade away by midnight and leave the revels to the boisterous young.

Parents kept pretty careful track of the young women invited, but as a successful dance needed three men to one girl, and as the parties had now swelled to a point where even a mansion couldn't contain them and a hotel ballroom in the city was required, hostesses had to consult professionals who kept lists of eligible young men if they wanted a lively evening. Faced with dozens of young males unknown to him, not to mention house guests roped in at the last moment and numberless crashers, the poor father of the debutante, far from imagining that his daughter might find a husband in the crowd, devoutly hoped she would have none of them.

What then was the point? Like many fashions it had none. Napoleon is supposed to have said, when his armies were occupying most of Europe, that if fashion wasn't with him in Paris he was nowhere. And to many girls, particularly those on the periphery of the social world, to whom college had not yet presented itself as a viable alternative to a year of dining and dancing, her party was everything.

Of course, the expense, now that an orchestra and a dance floor were essential even to a minor affair (not to speak of a tent and valet parking in the country), was a problem for even successful professional fathers, but few of them could face the tears and fury of a denied daughter.

I recall a Yale classmate who gave up his college career to help his parents with the expenses of his sister's coming-out party, but this, of course, was generally considered madness, and I cite it only to show how extreme a folly could wax.

I knew a beautiful and intelligent girl, the only child of elderly parents of old stock but sadly depleted fortune, who looked upon her party as the only means to restore her own and her family's position in the world—particularly her own. She badgered and bullied the poor old couple into using a valuable slice of their remaining capital to give her a large dinner dance at an elegant country club. During dinner, at which I was her partner, a vulgar clown, an unexpected and unplanned part of the divertissement, struck her suddenly and unreasonably as having ruined her party, and she sobbed for a hysterical moment, her hands over her face. But I soon persuaded her that actually the silly clown had amused her guests, and she quickly recovered. I had seen, however, what it meant to her. It appalled me.

The party opened up a life for her that seemed to be everything she had wanted. She married a rich and amiable man who bought her everything she desired, including an enormous diamond into whose brilliant interior she used to silently stare during the dismal months when she was dying young of a fatal cancer. What a subject for a Dürer etching.

Careers for women were talked about but rarely opted for by mothers of children or women of independent means. In my class at law school there were only three woman students, and in the older generation of my family an unmarried aunt who became a trained nurse was a great rarity.

All the better positions, of course, in the professions, except in teaching, writing, and drama, were the exclusive property of the male. In politics and diplomacy women were often noticed, but it was largely for their skillful use of purely female tools, such as charm and beauty. In the eighteenth century, a Madame de Pompadour could seriously influence her nation's foreign policy; today a Margaret Thatcher can use the same tools as a man.

A striking example of what a brilliant woman of my generation could accomplish and not accomplish in the diplomatic world may be seen in the career of Susan Mary Jay (later Patten and Alsop). When she wrote history with an emphasis on chatty biography, her shrewd observation and lively style gave her a success to which her sex was no impediment. But where her real ambition lay it was, which was to influence the great men of her time through the charm and fascination of her salon. She certainly succeeded in getting to know many if not most of the leading political leaders in Paris, London, and Washington, but what in the end did she really have to show for a lifetime of parties? Would she have been content to have had it written on her tombstone that she had given the only dinner party which Colin Powell had left his office to attend during the whole of the Gulf War?

Susan Mary's assets and liabilities for a career of constant affiliation with the great were evenly balanced. On the plus side she had looks and charm, and her social position, as a direct descendant of our first chief justice and daughter of an ambassador to the Argentine, was assured. Her family was not wealthy but comfortably off, with residences in town and country. On the liability side she suffered the loneliness of an only child with a bereft widowed mother who had lost a husband from a lingering asthmatic ailment. I remember in Bar Harbor summers in my boyhood visiting Susan Mary in the Jays' house on the beautiful Shore Path and hearing her poor father's incessant hacking cough from the second story. When I first met her charming but always ailing first husband, Bill Patten, and heard that same cough, I knew there had to be a romantic element in the pity and love it inspired in the woman exposed to it by parent and lover.

Starting in a minor government position with a constantly ill though always delightful spouse in the postwar Paris of 1949 hardly seemed the initiation for a great social career, but it was all Susan Mary, who saw all and forgot nothing, needed. She borrowed the perfect little house from rich and absent American cousins and trained a small staff to give perfect little dinners. She perfected her French and studied French history.

But perhaps *one key* to her phenomenal social success in the French capital lay in her cultivation of an intimate friendship with the famous and beautiful Lady Diana Duff Cooper, wife of the British ambassador and queen of Paris. Lady Diana had long tolerated her husband's mistresses, but she did this most comfortably when she chose them herself. Susan Mary was her prize; she did more than fall in love with Duff Cooper, she had a child by him. Everyone knew, and nobody seemed to care, including Bill Patten, who may have been gallant enough to feel that his illness entitled her to a less afflicted lover.

Certainly there was no romance in the second marriage that she contracted after Bill's long, expected, and sadly received demise. Joe Alsop, the famous political columnist, was a known homosexual, and Susan Mary knew all about it and totally accepted it. Here was her chance to be what she had always dreamed of being!

Nobody in Washington was too great to be asked to her dinner parties. Small and intimate evenings with the Kennedys in the White House were part of her social schedule. But fate can play cruel tricks on the most subtle of social climbers. Susan Mary had reckoned with Joe's tremendous charm but not with his terrible temper. What good does it do to a hostess to plan the perfect dinner party if she must see the guest of honor—be he a Supreme Court justice or cabinet member—reaching for his hat and leaving in a huff because he had just been insulted by Joe? Of course, the quarrel would be made up later—people were used to Joe—but the party was still in pieces.

* * *

These eruptions caused Susan Mary ultimately to seek an amicable divorce. Joe told me himself that he had assured Washington hostesses that he had no objection to appearing at parties to which his ex-wife was also asked. "Otherwise she would have had no invitations," he typically added.

The sad thing about Joe's characteristically egocentric remark was that it was perfectly true. Susan Mary had spent her life trying to be a kind of Joe Alsop, even to the extent of marrying him, but women in her day didn't have that kind of political influence. Their charm went just so far and no further. A generation later she would have used a man's tools. She might have even been a John Raben.

21

Animal Encounters

To BEGIN THIS DISCUSSION, which may be ill-
timed but which is meant only to be amusing—I must
zip back momentarily to childhood, when I never had a pet,
either cat or dog. Nor did I want one. During my childhood
there had always been one or two of the latter in the house, for
my mother loved them, particularly a beautiful boxer whom
she had to get rid of when it slit the throats of the two black
poodles of our next-door neighbor in Long Island, who was not
only a dear friend but the architect of our house.

Mother put the boxer in a kennel until it was time for us
to go to Maine, where she gave him to a farmer under condition that she could visit him every summer. The dog greeted
her ecstatically on each visit until there came one where she
was told he was dead. But driving away she heard him barking.
The farmer had been afraid she had come to take him back.

My parents thought it odd that I showed no desire for a
pet and thought I might be surprised and pleased if I found a
puppy as my principal present under the Christmas tree. But
I was only angry when told that because it was of an expensive

breed it was in lieu of several toys that I had asked for. And my anger turned to fury when the puppy made a mess and I was told I had to clean it up. My elder brother then offered to swap his copy of Martin Johnson's *Safari*, which I greatly coveted, for the puppy, which I refused because of the great difference in price. I ended up by being obliged to accept my brother's offer or nothing and told I had spoiled everybody's Christmas.

Well, I certainly hoped I had.

Another controversial present was given me by an eccentric aunt, a yellow and blue macaw whose huge and formidable beak so terrified me it had to be given to the Bronx Zoo where, considering their longevity, it may still be.

Although I never wanted another pet I loved going to the zoo and delighted in watching large dangerous animals safely locked away behind bars. This interest culminated in my adult years in two visits to see uncaged beasts in Kenya and Botswana. The latter country was then still so wild that some of the animals might never have seen a man, and I made a particular friend of our young guide David, who was a specialist in the wild dog, an endangered species. He had managed to make himself an accepted guest at the lair of a particular pack, and he took me there once when they returned from hunting, at always the same hour.

The dogs went about their business of feeding their young, forcibly if necessary, without paying us the slightest attention. "Do they even know we're here?" I asked.

"Watch me," he said and leaped out of the jeep. The whole

pack immediately jumped up, and he leaped back in. "They know our bargain," he explained.

Indeed they were almost human in their behavior. Or like the best humans, as David liked to point out. They killed only just what they needed and as quickly and painlessly as possible. When the two alpha females gave birth, the pack counted the litters, knowing just how many cubs they could support and rapidly killed the small surplus. The others were carefully nursed to survival even through serious ailments.

I still preferred elephants. I remember in Botswana looking for elephants in a small jeep bus containing five tourists and a guide. The latter was young and over-adventurous, for he was too close to a suspicious herd when we got stuck in long grass. The herd, led by a huge trumpeting cow, her ears flapping, besieged us in a tight little circle, and we thought our last day had come until the cow, diverted by our guide's odd yodels, decided we were harmless and let us go.

I really think I was not scared until it was over. I kept thinking, "Wow! I never thought it would all end this way!" And I remember, when the dreaded beasts had departed, asking the neat little silent old lady from Cincinnati who was sitting beside me, "Weren't you scared?" and her replying, "Mr. Auchincloss, to use a vulgar word, which I never do, I was scared shitless."

Theodore Roosevelt, though a remorseless hunter, was a great lover of wildlife and liked to speculate that some animals had morals. Certainly the wild dog had more than the lion. The king of beasts has been known to kill his own cubs to bring their mother back into heat for his pleasure.

Elephants are notorious for supporting their own sick and dying and are even believed to mourn their dead. In transporting one of them by air to a zoo, it is wise to prevent their dangerous stamping by placing small animals in their compartment, as they dislike crushing them. On the other hand they will kill a rhino for no reason at all, and a rogue elephant is always to be avoided.

I was not destined to have many contacts with dangerous animals, but the one I most recall did not occur in the wilderness but in the heart of civilization: London. It was during World War II and I was a naval officer on leave who was visiting, for no particular reason, the London Zoo. Many of the animals had been removed to escape the bombing, but when I passed the reptile house I asked a keeper if the dragon lizard of Komodo was still there and was surprised to hear it was. So I decided to go in.

I found the reptile house empty, with neither a visitor nor a reptile, except for one glass cage that contained the very monster I was seeking. It was moving back and forth, perhaps impatient for a delayed meal, and saw in me either the supplier or the meal itself. It even rose on its hind legs and approached the glass so that our heads were almost level. And then the silence was broken by the rattle of a V-1 flying bomb in the sky above. Of course I knew I was safe as long as the rattle continued; its stoppage would signify that the bomb was dropping. And then it stopped and I had a horrid moment of imagining myself and the beast facing each other over the soon to be shattered glass. But a distant detonation soon reassured me and I fled the reptile house.

My interest in this monster stemmed from childhood when I read *The Dragon Lizards of Komodo* by Douglas Burden, who led an expedition to the little-known Indonesian island where they had uniquely survived. He was a great naturalist and a romantic figure, remarkably handsome, as can be seen in the charcoal drawing of him made by Sargent for his mother when he went overseas in World War I. Happily he survived to bring home the bodies of the dragons so beautifully mounted in the diorama in the American Museum of Natural History.

In later life I knew Burden well, for I married his niece, Adele Lawrence, in 1957, four years after she graduated from Bryn Mawr. A rare and loving creature she was an artist and astonishing companion. I was luckier than could be imagined when she agreed to marry me.

Douglas Burden always behaved peculiarly about the dragons. He seemed to feel that because he had brought them to the attention of the greater public that they were somehow his property and that even scientists of repute should not mention them without giving credit to his role in their rediscovery. I could never convince him that the law gave him no greater rights in the beast than I had.

Part III

The Writing Life

◇◇◇

◇◇◇ 22 ◇◇◇

Writerly Types

M Y WIFE, THE FORMER Adele Lawrence, observed, in the first year of our marriage, 1958, that,
as by this time I had received some acknowledgment as a novelist, she had expected to meet more members of the literary
world. She did not say this with any particular disappointment;
her reading was mostly of detective fiction or works connected
with her passion: saving the natural environment.

Adele became the assistant administrator of New York City
parks and was a founding trustee of the Natural Resources De-
fense Council. She had simply assumed that writers would see
other writers, and had no objection to that. Indeed the odd-
ity of our very happy union was that our interests were almost
complete opposites.

"Is there some particular writer you'd like to meet?" I asked
her.

She didn't know many, so she picked a famous one. "Well,
what about Norman Mailer? You know him, don't you?"

"Certainly. And I happen to have an invitation from him in
my pocket. For Wednesday night."

"Fine. Let's go. What time and where?"

"His apartment's in Brooklyn. But there's no point getting there before midnight. It won't get started before then."

"Midnight! In the middle of the week! No thanks. We working folk will be beddy-bye well before that."

She understood thereafter why it was so difficult in that day for writers caught up in the workaday world to see their confreres socially. It was not only the hours; it was the heavy drinking then associated with creative writing that wasted so much time. In my bachelor days, and when I was not practicing law, I had ample time to meet, and did, some of the great literary figures of the time, and adapt myself to their hours. I can recall coming home at eight A.M. after an all-night drinking session with Jean Stafford and Philip Rahv and thinking nothing of it. As a married lawyer-novelist I soon changed my ways.

Childhood had not brought writers into my ken. The only one who came regularly to the house was my parents' great friend Arthur Train, author of the popular Ephraim Tutt stories about a wily but good-hearted old lawyer who didn't hesitate to misuse his legal genius to get an innocent man off the hook. But Train was no Thackeray. At Groton I read deeply in the British nineteenth-century classics: Dickens, Thackeray, the Brontës, George Eliot, but nothing contemporary, no Hemingway or Faulkner or even Fitzgerald. We were then living in an age where many believed that Galsworthy was the greatest writer in English and Anatole France the greatest in French. I passionately agreed with this evaluation until Proust crept into my life. But with him I preferred the social parts about the parties of the Guermantes. I thought his whole theory that love springs from jealousy was twaddle. As a matter of fact I still do.

I was still in my teens when a great change occurred in my parents' social life. Up until then the gatherings that they hosted or attended had been made up of old friends or relations, lawyer partners or business acquaintances, a congenial but very familiar group, rarely stimulating, never exciting. That changed when they were taken into intimate friendship (mostly because of Mother's wit and wisdom) by the four closely knit and infinitely interesting daughters of Walter and Margaret Blaine Damrosch. The doors of the world of music, theatre, and letters burst open for them. When they went out for dinner Mother might find herself discussing the filming of *Rebecca* with David Selznick or a revival of *Siegfried* with Lauritz Melchior or his days as a pianist in a whorehouse with Harpo Marx. Father enjoyed it too, and he was always charming and well liked, but he was less on top of it all than Mother, who had the advantage of feeling at her ease with even such a deity as Kirsten Flagstad.

The broadened social life of my parents made a good many famous names familiar in family chatter, but I cannot say that they had much effect on my early writing efforts. Their bearers simply nodded genially to a junior. I do remember reading the witty and vivid memoirs of Gretchen Finletter, the most intellectual of the Damrosch daughters, about her girlhood, and having a glimmer of how the simplest domestic things could be turned into art, but otherwise the whole business of writing seemed to me to have nothing to do with anyone but myself. It was only when I ceased to regard reading and writing as connected with grades at school and college, but as necessities to my pleasure in life, that they became really me. That was in my sophomore year at Yale in Joseph Seronde's class in nineteenth-century French fiction and drama.

This brings up the larger question of whether writers in general influence each other, the way painters do, as almost all art critics agree. I suspect that the major writers do not, or in a very minor way. Henry James is universally cited as an influence, but on whom? Who writes like him? Percy Lubbock, author of *Earlham*, is often given as an example, and the book is a good candidate, but it's largely a literary curiosity today.

I once deliberately tried to write an American counterpart to a favorite French novel of mine: *Renée Mauperin* by the Goncourt brothers. I even started it with the same scene of my heroine talking to a young man while bathing in a stream. But before many chapters were written my characters had taken over, and my novel was very different from its model. Not as good, of course, but different.

During the period of my life when I was free to meet other authors on their own terms I was guided by Vance and Tina Bourjaily who ran a kind of salon for just that purpose, which was ultimately transferred from their apartment to the larger space of the White Horse Tavern. Their eye was very good, for

I didn't meet anyone at their gatherings who didn't make some kind of a name for himself. Norman Mailer was their most famous regular. I had admired *The Naked and the Dead* a good deal more than I did its successors, but I was nonetheless dazzled to receive from him the greatest compliment one writer can give another. He said of my short story *The Gemlike Flame* that he wouldn't have minded writing it himself!

I found it difficult at first to win acceptance in the group. A registered Republican who was also listed in the Social Register was something of a duck-billed platypus to them. And by the time I had won a kind of welcome at the White Horse I found myself a little bit bored. Alcohol was certainly the bane of writers' meetings in those days, and it rarely improved the quality of the talk. I never had a really interesting conversation at the White Horse, though there were undeniably interesting people there. Perhaps I left too early, but I still doubt if any of the writers profited much from each other's company.

Do writers ever? Jane Austen, so far as we know, had no literary friends of any importance. Henry James had the most of all; he made a point of meeting every author of note in Britain, France, and America, many of whom sent him signed copies of their first editions so that his library when he died, though sold for a song by an idiotic niece, was worth a fortune. Would the late style of the three final novels have been altered in the least had he met none of the luminaries he cultivated? I doubt it.

It always surprises me that great authors don't get more personal satisfaction from their gifts. Some, of course, do and did.

Trollope, Dickens, Browning, and Tennyson were all reputed to be happy in their trade. And, as I have noted elsewhere, I believe that Shakespeare was in exuberantly high spirits when he finished *King Lear*. But I have to admit that Henry James, and in our day William Styron, suffered cruel and crippling depressions at the very height of their literary powers. And was Emily Dickinson happy when she dressed in white and kept a door between herself and the friends she talked to? Who knows?

23

Class

A S MY WRITING career advanced, it seemed that, aside from the specific preoccupations of the characters and the stories themselves, a particular preoccupation emerged: class. Given what I have told you so far about my life and upbringing, it would have been shocking had the subject not been one of my major concerns. Class, whether real or imagined, is a subject of interest in America far greater than its actual existence would seem to justify.

No doubt there are areas, particularly in the Old South or parts of New England, where families that have retained their original prominence in the same neighborhood for a few generations are still treated with marks of respect, but it rarely amounts to any considerable political or economic power. Certainly our colonial society, largely based on its British government, was a class society. Its upper class dressed differently than its lower, had a different accent in speaking, married and socialized within itself, and certainly expected to have the major hand in government. But soon dress became uniform; accent varied only with geography; intermarriage was common;

society was mixed. On what basis could any segment of the population claim it was an upper class?

I am not speaking of professions like the clergy or the military or the law but of a class, like the aristocracy or the peasantry or the bourgeoisie. You can't really point to one in the United States. But you can certainly point to plenty of angry resentment against any who claim, or seem by their conduct to claim, to be upper class. The battle for a classless society has been long essentially won but the survivors do not all know it. Jealousy and envy are still rife.

Anyone can claim to be middle class (no one would claim to be lower) but the natural successor to an upper class, if we had one, would seem to be the rich, for money can purchase a great deal of power in a commercial society. But millionaires are rarely popular, and billionaires even less so, and many of them are wisely inclined not to flaunt their wealth. Even if they were sufficiently united to form a class, it would not be a popular or formidable one. America would not care to be dominated by a vision of a line of marble palaces on the cliffs of Newport. The one thing that the rich share in common is apt to be the Republican Party.

I try to recall what traces of class remained in my New York boyhood in the decade following World War I. My most vivid memory is of the destruction of the mansions on Fifth Avenue, which were being sold by the generation following the one that built them and replaced by huge apartment houses. The heirs were now sufficiently socially secure as no longer to need to impress their neighbors with a French chateau or Italian palazzo, and preferred a flat to the bother of running a palace. The wrecking crew of the latter would sometimes allow pedestrians to wander through the doomed ground floor, and I had a nurse who loved to do that, so I had a memorable vision of this twilight of the gods. I suffered at an early age from what the French call *la folie des grandes maisons* and imagined that I was viewing the tragic fall of an empire.

Why did these magnates build so closely together, both in New York and Newport? There was, of course, the pleasure of visibly outdoing a rival, but I think it was more the need to be near someone who was like you. It is not always agreeable to stand out from the crowd and sometimes it is good to be free of the awkward questions that the uninitiated put to you. The very rich are particularly subject to intrusive interrogation about how they spend their money, which their equals spare them. It is the same way that royalties feel about people who want to talk about their rank. Queen Victoria once confided in a relative that she only felt truly at her ease with other royalties. And the exiled Grand Duchess Cyril, whose husband pretended to the Russian throne, told a friend who warned her that she was seeing the wrong people in Paris: "It's so hard to tell, you know. For us there's just us and the rest of you."

Was superiority of birth ever an important factor in any of the New Yorks in which I lived? When I was very young, old city families such as the Van Rensselaers or the Livingstons were certainly spoken of by my grandparents' generation with a certain respect, but that has largely disappeared, partly because history no longer celebrates the families so named and partly because immigrants wishing to identify themselves with their new nation have changed their names to theirs. The only semblance to class distinction that we still have is through wealth. That name and birth count for little is shown by the fact that being called Rockefeller would do you no good unless you were a rich Rockefeller or supposed to be one.

European titles of nobility were much valued by the daughters of the American rich in the nineteenth century, and by a steadily diminishing number in subsequent years, but that was always a kind of parlor game, never taken really seriously by the men. As a child I never thought that my native city was ruled by any identified class, though I was well aware that the downtown world of Manhattan contained a host of my family's relatives and friends who had a great deal to say in the running of the institutions that loomed large in our local life. But they had nothing to do with urban politics, public schools, the police or firemen, or indeed any of the infrastructure of the city. Indeed, they sent us to private day schools and out-of-state boarding schools and colleges.

In a way we were privileged guests of New York; we knew no more of the West side world of Leonard Bernstein's opera than a Californian. Nor did our families want to know more. When we went to Central Park, or even just to walk for exercise in the streets, we were guarded by nurses, or, if old enough to go alone, severely instructed never to talk to strangers. Of one thing we were always aware: that the city was fraught with danger.

If the poor inspired fear in a crowded, poverty-stricken city, the rich inspired not so much fear as the apprehension of condescension. A typical American will boil at the smallest hint that someone feels himself his social superior. This has lessened now, but when I published my first novels the literary establishment was full of liberal or even Marxist critics who wrote as if they were involved in a personal vendetta against characters of mine who struck them as belonging to an upper class that wanted to rule the world.

This hostility, oddly enough, seems to have gone down just as the stock market has produced billionaires whose megafortunes might seem to justify it. Maybe it is because the old poverty has been lessened.

24

Burdens

WILLIAM A. M. BURDEN JR., who had received his fortunes from so many ancestors, came to me with the project of my writing a book about that family financed by him. He was so grave and serious it was almost impossible not to mock him a bit.

"It's a wonderful idea!" I exclaimed. "It's the great American story, isn't it? You have the essential founder of the clan, Henry Burden, the poor Scottish immigrant who comes penniless to our shores and refuses to present any of his letters of introduction to tycoons till he's made his first million, and then he gives a dinner and hands each tycoon his unused letter. That really shows them, doesn't it? And then the horseshoes. Didn't he shod the whole Union army? And we won't ask any questions about the commander in chief being his son-in-law, will we? Nor about the long bitter litigation over management between his two sons that managed to transfer a hunk of the fortune to Joseph H. Choate.

"And didn't the family bring ruin on themselves and Troy by staying too long in horseshoes and ignoring the advent of the automobile? Did that put them out? No! Why? Because they learned what the Hapsburgs had learned. Nube! Marry! They resuscitated themselves neatly at the altar with not one but two Vanderbilt marriages, and Burden Beaux Arts mansions reappeared up and down Manhattan's East side. So what do we need to complete the American success story? But we have it! A crook! Joseph Burden went to jail for embezzlement in the nineteen thirties."

Bill was not amused. "I don't know who's going to write that book," he muttered. "But if I'm paying, it won't be you."

Maybe I was wrong. I might have had fun with it. It had some of the fun and contradictions of the weird American story.

William A. M. Burden Jr., the rich investor and art collector, was a double second cousin of Shiela Burden Lawrence, my mother-in-law. His grandfather was Isaiah Townsend Burden and hers was James Abercrombie Burden Jr., who were brothers and sons of Henry Burden, the ironmaster of Troy, New York. But if the fathers of William and Shiela were first cousins, so were their mothers: Mrs. William A. M. Burden Sr. had been born Florence Vanderbilt Twombly and Mrs. James Abercrombie Burden Jr. had been born Florence Adele Sloane, both granddaughters of William Henry Vanderbilt, once deemed the richest man in the world. His fortune, however, was not divided equally, or even equally *per stirpes*: the bulk of it was left to his two eldest sons. William A. M. Burden Jr., however, received a fortune independent of the Vanderbilts from his maternal grandfather, Hamilton Twombly.

Henry Burden had invented a machine that enabled its operator to make a horseshoe from an iron bar in four seconds. It was used by the federal armies during the Civil War, and was so envied by the confederates that Jeb Stuart instructed his raiders to be on the lookout for Burden horseshoes and pick them up wherever they could.

After Henry Burden's death in 1871 dissention over control of the company broke out between his two older sons, and one of them retained Joseph H. Choate as counsel. The great lawyer came up from New York to reconnoiter the situation and wrote gloatingly to his wife in 1889: "The Burdens are famous for protracted lawsuits. The father of these men had one about spikes that lasted for twenty years. And why should this one about horseshoes come to an untimely end?"

It didn't. The Burden ironworks continued, but on a steadily declining scale as late as the 1920s. The two grandsons of Henry Burden who reconstituted his fortune but not his business, James A. Jr. and William A. M. Jr., had the glorious good looks and athletic builds to aid them in their entry through marriage into the Vanderbilt clan in the 1890s. The company was finally liquidated in 1940. Soon only an abandoned office building remained like the "vast and trunkless legs of stone" of Ozymandias's statue, as a witness to past splendor.

His wife, Adele, however, was no compliant Victorian spouse. She loved her handsome husband but she did not for a minute believe that fate had endowed her with Vanderbilt millions to pine away in dreary Troy where he insisted on living while steadily losing money of which she had no need. She would get Whitney Warren to build her a mansion on Ninety-first Street that needed twenty-six servants to keep it up and Delano & Aldrich to do another for her on Long Island with a famous garden. Both are still standing, the New York house as part of the Sacred Heart School and the Long Island one as a golf club. James, however, continued with the family stubbornness or loyalty to occupy the Burden mansion and office in Troy several days a week while his wife and children stayed in New York City. She also had a house in Paris. As she told me once in her old age: "Some of my cousins were embarrassed to have so much more money than other people. I knew it was there to be enjoyed, and I enjoyed it." She was lively and charming, a first-class horsewoman, devoted to fox hunting, an imaginative hostess and a wonderful friend. But her marriage was certainly under the constant strain of a frequently divided residence. Years after the premature death of her husband she remarried, in her sixties, Richard Tobin, an old bachelor San Franciscan, president of the Hibernian Bank there and our minister to the Netherlands. She adored him and proved a more compliant wife, for she was converted to his Catholic faith and even spent her winters in California. But when she died at eighty-eight, she surprised her family by leaving instructions that she was to be buried in the Burden mausoleum in Troy. Was it repentance? Her children were chagrined to find the neglected marble mausoleum in such bad shape it had to be expensively repaired to receive her remains.

Adele left a diary covering her early twenties and first marriage that nobody had read and that I instantly saw as a document of some historical importance. With the family's consent

I took it to Jackie Onassis at Doubleday, with whom I had already worked on several publications. I soon convinced her that almost everything written about the opulent New York society of the 1890s was trash, and that here was the real thing: a bright and observant heiress of the richest and most famous clan describing the daily doings of that extravagant era. I also had family albums showing the individuals and mansions involved. George Vanderbilt, for example, had had the tower on Biltmore photographed every day of its construction and I could show it as it was on the very day the diarist came to visit.

But Jackie refused to be bound by my severe limitation of the illustrations to the dates and events described in the diary. When I would object to her including in the published book the picture of some great lady in fabulous fancy dress, pointing out that the party had been given after the diary ends, she would say, "Do we have to be so technical?" And then I learned that when you have as an editor a former first lady of the United States, you lose those arguments. And Jackie was right, too. The book was the portrait of an era.

25

A Would-be Writer, Not Forgotten

STUART PRESTON, who died at ninety, an expatriate president of Paris, is a name that one encounters not infrequently in the diaries and memoirs of noted society and literary figures, both French and English, of the 1940s and '50s. By the 1960s he was largely forgotten in the smart circles that he had frequented. It was not because people in the least disliked him or even disapproved of him; he was always kind and amiable and asked nothing of life but to be accepted by charming people who lived charmingly. He was certainly an elegant guest who fit comfortably and easily into the elegant homes where he was welcome. Why then was he more or less dropped by so many of the great ladies who had picked him up?

I think it was because they ultimately feared not that other people might associate them with Stuart, i.e. think they were like him—they were mostly too independent to care what others thought—but that they might begin to think so themselves. In other words, that his superficiality might be somehow catching. It was not a thing really dangerous, but it might be well to avoid, like a friend's head cold. Or it may be that they just tired of poor Stuart. Snobbishness can become tiresome, and a love of ancient titles and historic homes, however disguised (as in Proust) as a passion for history, always contains an element of snobbishness.

It was, however, undeniable that some of Stuart's most famous friends came to treat him with a bit of a sneer. Once when I reproached Nancy Mitford for a nasty remark she made about him, telling her I had thought Stuart was such a friend of hers, she had retorted: "Friend? Never forget, my dear, that we're a nation of warriors and don't number among our close friends young men who spent the war having tea with Sibyl Colefax." And Evelyn Waugh records in his journal of a New York meeting with Stuart: "Bald and waxy eyed. I suspect he drinks."

Despite what Nancy said about the war it was that great conflict that brought Stuart his greatest success. He came to London as an obscure American sergeant in the intelligence force, surely no social recommendation to a congregation of warriors accustomed to meet only commissioned officers, and was stationed there for several years with apparently very little to do. An English friend arranged to make him the guest of honor at a grand dinner celebrating the centennial of Henry James, casting him as the "Passionate Pilgrim," and somehow it took on. Stuart became the rage, known throughout the swellest London society as the "Sarge." He appears as "The Loot," an uncomplimentary picture of him in Evelyn Waugh's Sword of Honour trilogy.

He was a lifelong friend of mine and my family's, and I have never known quite how to assess his remarkable popularity and its equally remarkable collapse, his appeal to all sorts of brilliant men and women and his fading from the scene, always in good humor. He had been very handsome; the poet Stephen Spender called him the handsomest man he had ever known, but he lost his looks with age and baldness. He was gay, but very discreetly so. In all the years I knew him, we never discussed the matter.

A death notice gives an idea of his vogue.

His high moment of fame came when he was confined to a hospital with jaundice in March 1943. "The whole of London congregates around the Sergeant's bed," wrote Lees-Milne. "Like Louis XIV he holds levees. Instead of meeting now at Heywood Hill's shop, the intelligentsia and society congregate in public ward No. 3 in St. George's Hospital. When a visitor arrived late to see George VI, the King said: 'Never mind. I expect you've been to St. George's Hospital to see the Sergeant.'"

Stuart stemmed on the paternal side from obscure but respectable old New York stock, but his maternal grandfather was an Irish emigrant who became an important judge and millionaire and launched his vast tribe into society. The fortune ultimately disappeared in multiple divisions, but Stuart's small portion sufficed for him to live decently as a prudent bachelor. For some years he worked as a junior art editor, reviewing the minor shows perceptively, but never importantly. He tried to write books, but his attention span was too brief. His forte was the *mot juste*, the brief *apercu*. If you went to a gallery with him, and he was the perfect companion for this, and he brought something to your attention, it was apt to be funny or significant. I recall his nudging me to read this conscientious ticket under a vase in the collection of the duke of Wellington: "1817: Given to the first duke by Louis XVIII, King of France and Navarre. 1854: Smashed by Bridget Murphy, housemaid. 1855: Repaired by . . ."

Stuart died loved by those who appreciated what he had to offer, less so by the majority who always wanted more. Yet he resented nothing. His acceptance of life was perfectly cheerful.

Part IV

Farewells

◇◇◇

26

My Mother

TOWARD THE END of her life my mother—like my father—made no secret of the fact that I was her favorite child, explaining half-jokingly that I was the only child who realized that she, too, had once had a mother. A truer explanation would have been that I understood her better as the only offspring who had been through psychoanalysis.

John's early and extreme devotion to her had been soured in his later years because of her futile but persistent disapproval of his retirement at age fifty from the State Department and his choosing to live, however happily and comfortably, on the large fortune of his loving and beloved wife. Mother could never stop reproaching him in her mind for giving up a useful career, even when he was past sixty, and he and his wife were always conscious of this. "I detested your mother," Audrey told me after Mother's death.

My other brother, Howland, the youngest and most independent, was much less close to Mother, and his wife equally so, and my sister's lifelong struggle with manic depression created too tight a dependence on Mother not to lead to an ultimate resentment.

Certainly a part of the bond that united Mother and me was our extreme congeniality. We had similar tastes and laughed at the same things. I could tell simply by looking at her what she was thinking about a topic. I remember once when she wanted to show me a perfect example of her theory of how a miser fumbled when he had to open his purse, she excitedly poked me and pointed to the fumbler at the risk of self-betrayal. It was one of those instances when we seemed alone against the world.

In the early years of my marriage, my wife had some trouble accepting my closeness with my mother. But she soon and wisely made her own friendship with Mother, and at the latter's death she told me: "In some ways I'll miss her more than you will."

The painful split between Mother and me, which took some years to heal, was, as I have explained, over my writing. There was no avoiding it because my writing meant everything to me. If she could only have left me alone! But no. She was afraid that I was just slick enough to get my toe on the publishing ladder and would ruin my life and happiness as a hack. She felt it her duty to save me from such a disaster.

When Scribner's rejected my first novel and I foolishly resolved to write no more, and even to leave Yale without a degree and study law, she heartily encouraged me, riding roughshod over my father's sensible objections. Was it subconscious jealousy that made her seek to abort a literary career in her son which she, just as talented, had never allowed herself? Sometimes it seemed that she believed the province of the arts was not meant for the men of her family, that they were doomed, like my father, to law or business or medicine. Later on she strove successfully to abort a career in music for my brother and encouraged him to be the good doctor that he became. In that case, however, she was probably right. But she certainly never hesitated to interfere.

Mother was not a snob, though she tended to avoid those she considered the vulgar new rich, particularly in Bar Harbor —she did not seem to encounter them in New York—though it cost her children invitations to the more expensive junior parties. She had however a certain tribal loyalty to the sober and diminishing brownstone society of her parents, and this included a goodly number of highly fashionable families. This group was a bore to be in, as Oscar Wilde so ably put it, but a tragedy to be out of.

Mother could actually be astonishingly naïve about society. She insisted that people were kinder than one was apt to find them. She assumed that a noted Bar Harbor hostess would understand when she got out of a large formal dinner by pleading that it was too lovely an evening not to take the children on a picnic. The hostess regarded this as a near insult.

Much worse was something she did to Father's partners. My brother John in 1941 was being married to Audrey Maynard, whose widowed mother, Eunice, was quite awesomely richer than we. She lived in a splendid Ogden Codman French chateau on Long Island full of magnificent furniture and embellished by a great garden. Mrs. Maynard was old and ill and probably felt that her daughter's wedding reception was the last party she would witness (which it was) and wanted to have it particularly fine. In drawing up her guest list she exhibited a novel kind of snobbery. "No, I don't want Margaret Sloan," she was heard to observe. "She'll wear that ghastly green hat she's been sporting. It won't go with the house."

Mother constantly gave in to Mrs. Maynard where her own list was concerned, but trouble came with Father's twenty-some partners of whom Mrs. Maynard wished to include only John W. Davis, as he had been, as explained, a presidential candidate, and Frank L. Polk, a former assistant secretary of state. "I don't want my daughter's wedding to be an outing for the bar association," she observed. This was made more embarrassing by the fact that the groom was an associate in the firm.

My mother's solution of the problem made matters much worse. She hadn't the nerve to insist on the sanctity of her own list—after all it was Mrs. Maynard's house and party. But she thought if she wrote privately to the more important of the partners, explaining to them it was a small wedding, which it wasn't, and asking them, if they happened to find themselves in the neighborhood at the time, to stop in and drink the health of the bride and groom. She hoped that Mrs. Maynard would never notice a few extra faces in the crowd. Nor did she for there weren't any. The partners did not feel that they had received an invitation that would justify their intruding themselves on Mrs. Maynard's hospitality.

* * *

Mother's greatest blunder, at least so far as I was concerned, was in inducing me to bring out my first published book under a pseudonym as she feared the reaction at Sullivan & Cromwell. Why I weakly succumbed to her passionate plea that I at least use a pen name, I don't know. You would think that at age thirty, after four years of total absence from home on naval duty in Atlantic, Pacific, and Caribbean waters, I might have developed the independence to bring out my own book under my own name. And what made the whole thing even more ridiculous was that my friends all knew about the book anyway. The only point to a pen name is to conceal the true author, and the secret was already out. I had made a fool of myself.

The book was well reviewed, and none of my bosses gave a damn about it. But Mother, not in the least abashed, continued her fretful opposition to my publications, shifting her ground and claiming now that two characters in my next novel would give offense to my elder colleagues in law as libelous cartoons. It was years before Mother came around to my side, and I forgave her. What made me in the end do so was the sense that I was really the one to blame for giving in to her foolish obsession.

It is only fair to add that Mother would never have been so silly with any but a child. She had a neurotically exaggerated sense of the duty she owed her offspring, and she sought it in the most unlikely places. With the large host of her good friends she allowed her beautifully sound mind free play, and they came to her constantly for advice in the most private and personal matters. As one woman who suffered from her mother's opposition to her perfectly acceptable beau, a problem deftly solved by my parent, told me, "Thank God I wasn't your mother's child! I'd never have gone to her then for advice."

Where was Father in all this? Well, the blindness that Mother showed with her children did not exist with him. They adored each other, and she was genuinely helpful in the severe periodic depressions from which he suffered. If he intervened in a family matter she promptly deferred to him. What she feared was responsibility, and once he assumed it, she was only too glad to be unburdened. It is a great pity that he did not assume it more often.

It must not be assumed that Mother's occasional social ineptitudes had any serious effect on her wide reputation as a brilliant and attractive figure in the world. People thought of her as a much more forceful and self-assured person than she actually was. She had little appreciation of her own gifts, and when she wrote for a privately printed family genealogy an enchanting introduction about the lives of her parents' generation, she insisted that it be produced as a detachable pamphlet so that it could be thrown away and not clutter up the volume. She refused to see any merit in her writing. If she had only waited to be born in that son's generation, she might not have died with that talent unwasted.

The little piece I have mentioned, consisting of some dozen pages about her mother and aunts and uncles, is a beautiful picture of a closely knit upper-middle-class New York family of the 1890s and early 1900s. It is a kind of fable of how to combine worldliness and epicureanism with warmth, tolerance, and humanity, and live happily and attractively. I tried to catch some of its flavor in my novel *Portrait in Brownstone*.

In my first book, *The Indifferent Children*, I created a character based on a friend of mine who was a charming fellow but a bit of an ass. He recognized himself and was deeply hurt, and I resolved never to do that again. But when I came to write *Portrait in Brownstone*, based on Mother's family, I could hardly avoid resemblances, so when I took her the finished manuscript, I rather handsomely, I thought, offered not to publish it in her lifetime if she objected.

"Why should I mind?" she asked. "They're all dead. I rather like your bringing them back."

Portrait in Brownstone turned out to be a bestseller, as has often been the case with novels that are family sagas. *The Newcomes*, *The Forsyte Saga*, *Buddenbrooks* come instantly to mind. The novel form suits them exactly. It provides the smoothest method of changing the theme with each generation to which there can be no objection. The son of a saint can be a serial killer if the author wishes, or even another saint.

Many literary critics like to play the game of seeking out the actual person who they imagine was the model from whom an author has copied a particular character. Some of them credit the author with no imagination whatsoever; he is always hiding a source. It is a harmless game but rarely contributes much to the understanding or even the appreciation of the work involved. Some authors are obvious copyists; others are not. It doesn't affect their quality. We can find a model for almost every character in Charlotte Brontë's fiction; none in Emily's. Both were great writers. Sometimes a writer may use more than one model for a character; several great ladies have been perceived in Proust's Duchesse de Guermantes. In my own case I always start with a particular person in mind, but as my story develops he or she may change in character, appearance, virtue, age, or even sex, though the latter is very rare.

One thing a writer must learn is not to be surprised by the curious identifications that readers constantly make. The best-known character of all my books, the headmaster in *The Rector of Justin*, my number-one bestseller and winner of a national prize, which still annually sells many copies, has been almost universally seen as modeled on the Reverend Endicott Peabody, a gentleman who shared not a single characteristic with my rector. But they were both headmasters, were they not? And Auchincloss went to Groton, didn't he?

What makes this even odder is that, more than any other character in my fiction, I *had* modeled my rector on an actual person, the late Judge Learned Hand, the greatest man I ever knew, and whose personality was not only publicly known but the very opposite of Peabody's.

◇◇◇ 27 ◇◇◇

And Please Do Not Forget

W HO CAN SAY why some are born inside the circles that some consider of such importance and why others are placed in less advantageous positions. I cannot, but I wanted to give a special prominence to one memorable personality who loomed large in my early years, despite her being neither actual family or of shared background. You see, no one—in society or in any of the grand, monied places I have seen—is more etched in memory than Maggie Kane. She came to us fresh from a poverty-stricken Ireland. I believe my parents were her first and perhaps her last employers—but she never showed the attachment or homesickness for the old country that our other Irish maids did. She was very young when she left and perhaps it was not a happy home that she chose to forsake.

At any rate she never referred to it. Nor did she ever really adopt America or American ways. The world that she accepted with seeming totality was simply the world that we as a family offered her: our household of family and servants in a New York brownstone, a country house on Long Island, and a seaside villa in Maine. In these she spent a whole lifetime until the day she left us—or disappeared rather, for we never found her—perhaps in her sixties. The detective we hired to locate her thought she had returned to Ireland, but I never thought so. Years later we received a package containing photographs of me and my siblings that I knew she had had. It had been mailed in the New York area. It may have come from people with her when she died. We never knew. She felt, poor soul, that she had survived her function in our lives: the children she had lovingly nursed were all grown and had their own independent existences; the parents were old and well looked after; her position in the household was a kind of charity. She knew she was loved and was welcome to remain as a kind of pensioner, but her pride required her to remove herself.

The life of those poor Irish immigrant girls in the 1920s and '30s was not an enviable one. They frequently came alone, leaving families glad enough not to have to support them further, and went into domestic service here for which there was a constant demand but which was badly paid and futureless. They were apt to be relegated to tiny rooms at the top of big houses to which the heat sometimes didn't reach and share a bathroom with four or five other housemaids. They had a day off each week, but what could they do with it? They knew nobody and had no means of meeting people, and if they were lucky enough to have a boyfriend (a "follower" as they were somewhat contemptuously referred to by employers) he was certainly not welcome in the house where they served. When the family in summer moved to a country place it was apt to be near some village where the locals were totally uninterested in the visitors' Irish help.

When we went to Maine my mother was actually heard to say that the maids should be happy in the beauty of Mount Desert Island, but what did they care about that? The sea by our house was really too cold for any but the hardy to bathe in, and anyway the poor maids were scared of sharks. Their sole diversion was on Saturday afternoons when the chauffeur might drive them to the village of Bar Harbor where they could see a movie as racy as Pola Negri in *DuBarry, Woman of Passion*.

Maggie's official position with us was as a nurse to my sister and me. My elder brother didn't need a nurse, and my younger one had his own, a huge Swedish woman who looked after Priscilla and me on Maggie's day off. We never had a governess who would have been addressed as "Miss" and taken her meals with our parents. Maggie ate with the other maids in the servants' dining room. But she soon developed the entire trust of both my parents and assumed the undisputed position of a general family adviser. She had a wonderfully deep and realistic common sense that was badly needed at times to moderate Mother's occasional volatile and nervous thinking where her offspring were concerned. When we heard Maggie's impassioned but always respectful cry to a bizarre suggestion of Mother's—"Woman, dear, are you mad?"—we knew that plans were going to be changed.

Yet Maggie never encroached on her favored position in

the household to lord it over the other maids or even to obtain some special privilege for herself. She was utterly content with the status quo and never wanted to change it by an iota. She loved us children as if we had been her own, but I don't think she ever caused my mother a moment of maternal jealousy. She comforted her in her sadness at sending us to boarding school. "Your poor mother is so upset at sending you off," she told me. "In this country you have to be rich to afford the unhappiness of parting with your children."

Maggie gave physical proof of her devotion to her wards. One afternoon when Priscilla and I were little and coming back from the park, each holding on to one of Maggie's hands as we crossed a street under a green light, a taxi that had failed to stop completely at the red lurched toward us, and Maggie instantly hurled us both onto the safety of the sidewalk, receiving herself the blow of the impact. Fortunately she soon recovered.

Maggie made friends easily enough with other Irish nurses at the Bar Harbor Swimming Club and sometimes for our amusement and sometimes perhaps for our improvement let us know what was said about us. My parents had an argument as to which came out on top in this assessment of Maggie's acquaintance. "The nurses say that Mrs. Auchincloss seems so cross, and Mr. Auchincloss is so pleasant spoken, but I tell them if they knew them better they'd find it is just the other way round." It was true that Mother, when occupied with her own thoughts, had a preoccupied look that could be interpreted as bad humor, and Father's social manners were always charming, but it was also true that in the home Mother's nature was almost invariably equable and Father could be sharply impatient.

Maggie's conversation was full of odd quotations that she would insert into the general discourse when she deemed relevant, which seemed to have come from some unrecognizable body of folklore, like "'I see,' said the blind man, when he couldn't see at all," but they were vivid and made us laugh. Mother and Father didn't believe in corporal discipline, and we were never spanked, but this didn't stop Maggie in what she regarded as a necessary means of correction. But she was never violent, and we would have died rather than betray her to Mother. We always adored her, and my sister's ultimate decision not to have her as a nurse for her own children, the relationship being too close, I always resented. It would have been the ideal solution for the problem of Maggie's later years.

These were not easy. As we grew up Maggie's function as a nurse disappeared. There was never any idea of letting Maggie go; she had become too much a part of our lives, and in a large household there were always tasks that she could perform: cleaning, mending, darning, tending anyone who was sick, walking the dogs, and so forth. But the time came when the children were all gone and Mother and Father moved to smaller quarters and really there was nothing to fill Maggie's time. Most painful of all as I recall it was Maggie's desire to keep up with all our doings and new interests, which she was unable to share. The truth was that there was really nothing for

Maggie and us children to have a serious talk about. Hugging is not enough. But even now, many years later, after I have lived more than ninety years, Maggie remains someone to recall, not a subject for a writer of my ilk, as it happens. Rather, a genuine and lasting comfort.

EPILOGUE

Words

◇◇

It was a pity that none of my students in the three years I taught at NYU seemed to have any real conception of the beautiful language that was theirs. I do not think it helped that most of them had never had a lesson in grammar. Yet classes in what is called creative writing are offered in colleges from coast to coast to students who couldn't explain to you the use of the subjunctive. It is not that they can't learn. They are quick enough. It's that grammar is not a glamorous subject.

In reading a student's paper I frequently had to ask: "This sentence—do you mean A or B?"

The student would look at it. "Why A, of course."

"Read it for B."

"Oh."

"Now let's rewrite it so it can mean only A."

The student would do it! They *wanted* to be taught!

Some years ago I received an honorary degree from SUNY Geneseo, one of our sixty-five New York campuses, and as I knew the president I stayed with him for a bit and got briefly to meet some of the faculty and students. I found them lively and stimulating and the campus quite as attractive as Yale's. I could not see that it lacked any advantage or opportunity that I enjoyed in New Haven, and, had I gone there, I believe I would have made interesting friends and been just as well taught, and at a small fraction of the Yale cost.

It so happened that the head of all sixty-five of the state campuses was attending the Geneseo graduation that spring, and I had the privilege of a long talk with him. When I asked him why so many families virtually impoverished themselves were paying the heavy tuition of the private college when SUNY offered the same for so much less, he replied with one word: fashion.

There was another factor in the romantic glow in which so many college graduates bathe their undergraduate years. They forget that those were the years when their souls were just awakening to the beauty and challenge of the world around them. At Yale to hear Professor Chauncey B. Tinker, in a low, half-broken voice, bewail the tragic deaths of Keats and Shelley was a moving and dramatic highlight that a few years later might have struck me as a bit hammy.

Great lecturers seldom hesitate to use dramatic tricks to enshrine their precepts in the minds of their audiences, and at Yale perhaps Chauncey B. Tinker was the most noted. To read one of his lectures was like reading a monologue of the great actress Ruth Draper—you missed the main point. You missed the drop in his voice as he approached the death in Rome of the tubercular Keats; you missed the shaking tone in which he described the poet's agony for the absent Fanny with whom his love had never been consummated; you missed the grim silence of the end.

Yet Tinker could be fussy and imperious in the classroom. You were allowed in only if you were enrolled in his course for credit. If your schedule had not allowed this, but you wished to sit in the back of his classroom and hear him lecture for your own edification—no luck. He didn't give a damn about your edification. He would start his lectures by having us write a ten-minute paper on a given theme. At the end of the hour he would collect these, all written on the same-size paper he had handed out. Once I had the misfortune to have used a larger paper that wouldn't stack neatly with the others that he collected, and he yanked it out and tossed it impatiently back at me. When I brought it back to him, recopied on the right paper, he accused me of making a mountain out of a molehill.

Though odd and crotchety he was deeply popular with the leading undergraduates: the members of the better senior societies, the signal athletes, the editors of the *Yale News*. Brendan Gill wrote a memorable story about him, where the young protagonist at Yale, snobbishly ambitious to join the "right" undergraduate circles, ignores his father's advice to cultivate an old professor and paternal friend who strikes the son as a social dead end, and wastes his time rapping on doors that remain closed. Admitting his failure as graduation nears, he calls in a fit of repentance on the paternal friend whom he has neglected and meets there all the men who have snubbed him! He has missed his golden chance.

I will leave you with that. Society matters not so much. Words are everything.